KARATE
BASIC MANUAL

KARATE
BASIC MANUAL

A. Pfluger

STERLING PUBLISHING CO., INC.   NEW YORK

Other Books of Interest

All About Judo
Complete Book of Karate and Self
  Defense
Junior Karate
Karate for Young People
Kung Fu for Young People: The Ving
  Tsun System
Mas Oyama's Essential Karate
Sports Acrobatics

Translated by Manly Banister

Published in 1982 by Sterling Publishing Co., Inc.
Two Park Avenue, New York, N.Y. 10016
The original edition was published in Germany under the title "Karate" by Falken-Verlag E.
Sicker KG, Wiesbaden. First English-language edition published in hardcover
under the title "Karate Kiai!" © 1977 by Sterling Publishing Co., Inc.
Distributed in Australia by Oak Tree Press Co., Ltd.
P.O. Box K514 Haymarket, Sydney 2000, N.S.W.
Distributed in the United Kingdom by Blandford Press
Link House, West Street, Poole, Dorset BH15 1LL, England
Distributed in Canada by Oak Tree Press Ltd.
c/o Canadian Manda Group, 215 Lakeshore Boulevard East
Toronto, Ontario M5A 3W9
Manufactured in the United States of America
All rights reserved
Library of Congress Catalog Card No.: 82-50553
Sterling ISBN 0-8069-7654-3

CONTENTS

In Karate you often see opponents using force while holding their breath. Many Judokas also hold their breath at the moment of the greatest development of strength (at the beginning of a throw). However, from a medical viewpoint, this is usually considered unhealthy. In addition, it is not very efficient. We know today, after an extensive series of experiments carried out by sports physicians and physiologists that the greatest force is developed at the point when half the air in the lungs has been expelled. You must have at some time experienced this fact yourself. For example, you may have had to lift a heavy object from the floor to the table. You take hold of it, but it is so heavy you can hardly lift it from the ground. What do you do? You tense all your muscles, you exert yourself and involuntarily you gasp—you inhale deeply, and then you exhale. All of a sudden you can lift it up quickly. In the course of doing this, you exhaled part of the air that you were previously compressing, and in doing this you helped your muscles to tense. This is the main reason for uttering the battle cry of Karate, "KIAI," which helps to attain your maximal body tension at the moment of striking.

Foreword

Karate, as it is practiced today, is an art of combat achieved by training all of the limbs, both arms and legs, as natural defensive and attack weapons. Fists, the edges of the hands, elbows, knees, and feet are effectively brought into action to strike, punch, and kick. Moreover, in fighting practice, the heaviest attack must be braked or arrested shortly before body contact. This naturally requires the most extreme body control and self-discipline, which can only be achieved by long years of diligent training.

This book is concerned only with the basic techniques of punching *(tsuki)*, kicking *(keri)*, and parrying *(uke)*. In relation to these basics are shown many combinations for sports competition. In addition, the *kata*, or the "grammar," of karate is discussed in detail and illustrated in photo sequences. Also included are some methods of giving immediate attention to injuries that may occur, though rarely, in karate sports competitions. These methods are taken from the *kuatsu*, an ancient Japanese art of resuscitation which every karateka should know. Also, an appendix contains a program of karate training along with the rules of karate examinations and a glossary of valuable Japanese karate terms.

The author's first book, "Karate: Basic Principles" (Sterling Publishing Co., 1967), illustrates all the techniques in karate. The basic techniques are clarified by numerous photographs and all the striking techniques (edge of the hand, elbow, and so forth) are explained in detail. Step-by-step tips for self-instruction are also given along with the rules of competition and a glossary of the most useful Japanese karate expressions. For this reason, the first book can be used as a basic text in conjunction with this book on perfecting your power. It can be considered a valuable reference as it points out in detail the essence of true karate.

Illus. 1. Gichin Funakoshi, founder of modern karate.

Before You Begin

Nowadays, karate is practiced from three points of view: as self-defence, as a sport, and as a way to physical and mental mastery of the "self." Serious practitioners, however, stress that the true essence of karate lies far deeper than the level of mere defensive tactics. Karate, if studied seriously and carried on responsibly, is first of all a means of training in the various shades of meaning of the saying:

"The uppermost goal in the art of karate is neither victory nor defeat—the true karate fighter strives for the perfection of character."*

Karate, nevertheless, has been known longest as a means of self-defence. It has its roots in the 2,000-year-old Chinese form of boxing called *Ch'uan fa (Kung fu)* or *kempo*, which is still practiced in China today. Around the year 1600, a fighting art was developed on the island of Okinawa which was then already in cultural contact with China and Japan. This art of fighting called *Okinawa-te* (Okinawa-hands) was a combination of *kempo*, brought in by Chinese soldiers, and the native style of fighting. In the political reshuffling that beset Okinawa, its inhabitants were forbidden by their rulers to carry any arms whatsoever. As a result, *Okinawa-te* became sweepingly popular as a secret art of self-defence. This art was kept so secret that in contrast to the Chinese *kempo*, there exist no historical records regarding old *Okinawa-te*.

Around the turn of this century, when the value of the fighting art *Okinawa-te* for cultural education was recognized on Okinawa, the art was introduced into the lower grade secondary schools. Then, the name *karate* was chosen to replace the name, *Okinawa-te* (Illus. 2). In this name, the first written character *(kara)* means China, so that the translation at that time meant something like "Art from China" (more literally, China-hands).

---

*Note: Detailed observations on the theme of Education Through Karate are contained in the basic book, "Karate: Basic Principles."

The man who deserves credit for having developed today's world-renowned karate is Gichin Funakoshi (Illus. 1), an inhabitant of Okinawa. He undertook journeys to Japan, where the ancient arts of war were experiencing a great rebirth—the development of *jiu-jitsu* into *judo*, the rise of the Japanese *kendo*, and

Illus. 2   Illus. 3

so forth. With his demonstrations (1917 and 1922), he gathered a large following and was remunerated for teaching his art in Japan. He travelled about the country to give instructions and exhibitions and many large universities asked him to help in the training of karate groups. Later on, Master Funakoshi would confine himself to Japan to systematize karate from scientific viewpoints, similar to the way the Japanese scholar J. Kana developed the old *jiu-jitsu* into *judo*. The systematization

Illus. 4. Gichin Funakoshi at the age of 88.

of karate also made it possible later on to conduct competitions that were free of danger.

When Funakoshi went to Japan, the Japanese fighting arts of *jiu-jitsu (judo)* and *kendo* were being ardently practiced there. Karate soon took over many elements of these two arts, and thereby the cornerstone for the development of today's modern Japanese karate was laid. Later, Funakoshi changed the name of his new art of fighting from China-hands to "empty hands" (Illus. 3). The written character for "empty" or "unarmed" is also read *"kara."* The character for "hand" or "hands" remained the same.

The karate style invented by Funakoshi is called *Shotokan**, the best-known and most popular style both inside and outside Japan. Funakoshi, who died in April, 1957, at the age of 88, chose this name after the building in Tokyo where he gave instructions. This he did in order to distinguish his karate method from others which had sprung up in the meantime (Illus. 4).

---

*NOTE: "Karate: Basic Principles" fully describes the *Shotokan* style. This new book brings out additional fighting combinations for competition.

13

Illus. 5. "The Cat."   **Illus. 6. Chojun Miyagi.**

As karate went through a great upswing in Japan, still other masters of the art were soon attracted from Okinawa and China to give instructions. Following this, there developed in Japan a mixture of other karate methods which did indeed often differ from each other in technique, but in essence remained the same.

The best known today are *Shito-ryu, Goju-ryu*, and *Wado-ryu (ryu* = school). *Shito-ryu* was established in 1930 by Kenwa Mabuni who came to Osaka from Okinawa. A few years later, Chojun Miyagi brought his *Goju-ryu* to Kyoto (Illus. 6). One of his most gifted students was a young man who wore his hair long in the fashion of the *samurai*, the Japanese knights of old. He was Gogen Yamaguchi, who today is leader of the *Goju-ryu* and is world-famous and highly esteemed under the name of "The Cat" (Illus. 5).

In 1935, Hironori Otsuka (Illus. 7), one of Funakoshi's students, founded a group of his own which he called *Wado-ryu (wado* = the Way of Peace). Technically, there is hardly any difference between *Wado-ryu* karate and Funakoshi's *Shotokan* style.

In October, 1964, at the initiative of the Japanese government, the largest karate clubs (Japan Karate Association, Shotokan, Wado-ryu, Shito-ryu, Goju-ryu) and several others were combined into the so-called "All-Japan Karate-do Federation." Today, however, this is only a name. Every single club still works for itself, bandies its own name about, and gives its own championship matches. It is still to be seen how far the single Japanese clubs can put aside their individual efforts in order to arrive at a common unity, which is something to be hoped for in the interest of all karateka.

The situation in America is similar. There are very many individual clubs, and unification is not in sight. In Europe on the other hand, a big collective movement can be observed. In France, the European Karate Union (EKU) which was founded some time ago has combined with the European Judo Union. Many European

Illus. 7. Hironori Otsuka.

countries are already members of the EKU and new members are enlisting at a steady rate. For this reason, championship matches have been held since 1966.

Korea is another country for which the term "split up" is no longer appropriate. During the period of the Japanese occupation, various karate-like fighting systems were formed, all of which were a combination of Japanese karate and the old Korean fighting art, *T'aekyon*. From this old *T'aekyon* (in which principally the feet were used) other systems had already been formed under Japanese and Chinese influence in which the hands were also used: *Tang-su* (= China hand), *Kong-su, Karate, Kwon-pop, Tae-su*, and so on. A few years ago in Korea, a successful unification was reached under the new name of *Tae-kwon-do*. This name expresses the fact that both hands and feet are used, while karate, somewhat incomplete, meant only "with empty hands." The creator of this new name was the Korean Choi Hong Hi, today a general and 9th Dan *Tae-kwon-do* who, during the period of the Japanese occupation, studied karate in Japan and deeply influenced the development of *Tae-kwon-do*.

The examples of France and Korea show that, undoubtedly, the future of all Japanese *budo* (knight) types of fighting sports *(judo, karate, aikido, kendo)* outside of Japan lies not in splinter groups but in unification.

Illus. 8. Hidetaka Nishiyama 6th Dan, smashes a block of three solid boards with *gyaku-tsuki*. (Photo by Charles E. Tuttle Co., Tokyo)

I. Techniques

Body Tension

There is nothing stiff about karate. It is an uncommonly dynamic art. Karate is not characterized by angular, strength-glorifying movements of only the arms and legs but by catlike, supple movements of the entire body with elastic use of all the limbs in defence and counterattack. For this reason, a good karate technique must develop suppleness in the hips, elasticity in the legs, and the capability (in connection with both) of displacing the body weight with lightning speed in defence and counterattack. Karate is the mastery of bodily tension—of relaxation as well as strain. As a karateka one learns, for this reason, to join the hard with the soft, not only in one's technique but also in one's attitude towards humanism and character. (In the name *Goju-ryu, Go* means hard or strong and *ju* means soft.)

In karate, movements must be quick as lightning. Therefore, the karateka must be physically and mentally relaxed to be able to react with lightning speed and execute the required movements. At the moment of striking, whether in defence or attack, all the muscles of the body are tensed as much as possible in order to concentrate the strength of the entire body into the moment of impact.

"Karate is speed turned into strength." To put it more clearly, "the energy of movement (kinetic energy) is changed into the energy of deformation." The greater and sooner kinetic energy is applied, the greater can be the result of the energy of deformation upon stopping. More simply, the faster your technique is, the greater the effect that can be felt by the opponent. I used the word "can" on purpose for speed alone does not make for the effect of a karate technique, although it is the prerequisite for it.

"Karate is the energy of motion changed into the energy of deformation." Thus, in the same moment that your technique has developed its greatest speed, stop suddenly. The change from energy of motion to energy of deformation occurs more completely the more successful you are at stopping without delay. This can be done only by the lightning-fast and extremely powerful straining of the muscles. This is the main reason why in karate one learns how to stop with hairlike precision. This is not because one does not wish to strike his partner while practicing, but because the unleashed energy is much greater than in a "shoving" punch, a punch without a "focal point" (Japanese *kime*).

In the case of a shoving punch, only a part of the energy of motion is converted into the energy of deformation. The greater part of the energy is conveyed to the one struck only as energy of motion, so that the effect of the shoving punch sets him in motion, thrusts him away, etc. With the karate punch, the one struck is not thrust away, but collapses on the spot. The shoving punch has still another disadvantage: if one does not hit the target, he falls out of balance—his own punch "pulling" him forward.

It is shown in karate that a concentrated and simultaneous working together of many muscles is more effective than an equally powerful working of individual muscles. However, in order to stop the arm in the course of punching with the fist, the strength of the arm muscles is sufficient. Why then strain all the other muscles when it appears that just the arm muscles are enough? We must go a little deeper into the mechanics of hitting or punching.

Recoil

With every blow or punch against an obstruction, the obstruction "strikes" back and, indeed, the more stable the obstruction, the harder it strikes back. You can feel that quite plainly in your hand. When you have tensed only the muscles of the aggressive arm, the entire back-thrust force or recoil exhausts itself in the rest of your relaxed body as a consequence. The recoil is "consumed" in your body—your hand is injured, your arm doubles up, possibly even your entire body is pressed backward.

Hence, you must achieve through karate technique the ability to impart to the struck object the entire energy released by the sudden, powerful stop. The recoil can be worked out especially with leg techniques. For this reason, in all leg techniques, the weight-bearing leg must cling to the ground with the entire sole of the foot and be slightly bent in order to be able to ward off recoil when striking.

There are two factors which help impart to the struck object the greatest possible amount of released energy without damage to your own body. These are:

1. Security of Footing

The lower the center of gravity and the larger the area in contact with the ground, the greater the security of footing. Karate positions are almost all low and wide. Moreover, they make it possible for the bodily tension in defence and attack (concentrated for the purpose of the moment) to be most highly effective in providing better security of footing in the direction required at any given time.

2. Bodily Tension

So that the force of the back-thrust (recoil) at the moment of striking cannot be dissipated, every muscle in the body must be tensed as much as possible during the short moment of striking. The stronger this tension of the entire body at the moment of impact, the more you succeed in passing on the released energy to the struck object. As the body becomes "rock hard" all over, the back-thrust (recoil) finds no point of attack and no possibility of being absorbed. The force passes through the entire body and is reflected again by the area of footing to the striking point (point of impact) (Illus. 8). Upon striking, the entire body is again relaxed and ready for the next technique.

The connection between tension and foundation (stance) and the tension of the technique (for example, the fist punch) lies in the lower abdomen*, the *hara*. The correct tension in the lower abdomen is very important in all techniques. Breathing helps here. In performing all techniques, exhale forcibly. Exhaling forcibly helps the muscles to tense up. This is the main reason for uttering the karate battle cry *kiai*, which helps you attain your maximum body tension at the moment of striking.*

Practicing Karate Techniques

Learn by progressing from relaxation to tension. This is the most important principle in practicing all karate techniques. In the beginning, do not put any force into the practice of individual techniques but work completely relaxed and thereby feel how the entire body, especially the hips, takes part in every technique. Not until the correct start of a movement (in the entire body) has been thoroughly mastered can you practice using force, the application of which is limited only to the moment of impact.

Karate Stances

In order to muster all the basic ingredients that go into an effective karate technique (recoil, bodily tension, etc.), the starting position or stance must be constructed with utmost precision. Stance is the method by which one organizes the power source in preparation for the limbs' smooth delivery of force from the source to the target.

*NOTE: In "Karate: Basic Principles" breathing, *hara*, and *kiai* or battle cry, are discussed in detail.

Hachiji-dachi, the basic stance (Illus. 9)

The feet are about a shoulder-breadth apart, the knees are slightly bent. The entire body posture is loose and erect.

Illus. 9   Illus. 10

Musubi-dachi, the linked-feet stance (Illus. 10)

The heels are touching; the feet point outwards at a 45° angle. The standing greeting *(ritsu-rei)* is executed in this stance.

Zenkutsu-dachi, the forward stance (Illus. 11 and 12)

One foot is thrust forward two shoulder-breadths (80 to 100 cm. or 32 to 39 inches), toes pointing directly forward. To be more exact, the edge of the foot points directly forward so that the foot is turned slightly inwards. Seen from the front, the legs are about a shoulder-breadth apart. The leg in front is sharply bent, the lower leg vertical and bearing about 60 per cent of the bodyweight. The back leg is stretched out straight and bears about 40 per cent of the bodyweight. In order to get the entire body under a state of tension which is concentrated in a frontal direction, the toes of the back foot are turned forward as far as possible. In doing this, pay attention that the soles of both feet are flat on the floor and in firm contact with it.

Kiba-dachi, the straddle-leg stance (Illus. 13 and 14)

Distribute the bodyweight equally on both legs. This causes the toes of both feet

Illus. 13         **Illus. 14**

to turn slightly inwards and the knees to press powerfully outwards. This stance stores up a large amount of tension and provides extremely strong support.

Kokutsu-dachi, the back stance (Illus. 15 and 16)

This is used especially in defence. The back leg is sharply bent and bears 70 per cent of the bodyweight. In this stance, the heels should be in line when viewed from the front. Illus. 17 shows a back stance shortened still more *(nekoashi-dachi)*, in which the forward leg is almost entirely free of bodyweight and touches the ground only with the ball of the foot.

Illus. 15

Illus. 16

Illus. 17

Notice in all the stances that the posture is loose and low, yet uncramped. It can be clearly seen here that the center of gravity does not lie in the thorax but in the lower abdomen *(hara)*. You must also constantly keep in mind that every technique and every movement must start from this center of gravity. Since both direction and strength are maintained from this center, always hold your body erect, with the shoulders relaxed and the tension concentrated in your lower abdomen *(hara)*.

Punching Techniques (Tsuki)

Punching is one way of delivering power from its source to the target and is therefore among the most common movements by the arms. The straight fist punch in karate strikes with the front side of the fist *(sei-ken)*. The striking points are thus the knuckles of the index and middle fingers (Illus. 18). So as not to sprain the wrist in striking, the fist must be aligned with the wrist (Illus. 19). When viewed from the side as well as from above, the straight line of the forearm passes through the two knuckles.

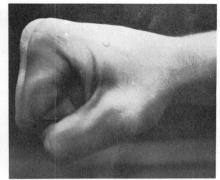

Illus. 18   **Illus. 19**

In school practice, the fist starts from the hip. Press the elbow inwards towards the spine and leave the other hand loosely outstretched. Punch towards the middle of the body and in doing so, turn the fist about 180° at the last moment. Simultaneously, draw the other hand back to the hip, turn it at the same moment as the punching fist, and close it into a tight fist. By drawing back this hand and powerfully closing it into a tight fist at the hip, the opposing force is carried over into the punching fist. This frontal punch is used in karate in connection with several techniques.

Oi-tsuki (also Jun-tsuki), the lunge punch (Illus. 20 to 24)

In moving forward in *zenkutsu-dachi*, the fist strikes its target at precisely the same moment the forward leg is moved forward. The high point of tension in the

Illus. 20

Illus. 21   **Illus. 22**   **Illus. 23**

lower abdomen (stance) falls in with the technique *(tsuki)* and makes it extremely effective. Tension both in the stance and in the arm technique must be connected

Illus. 24

through the *hara*. For this reason, exhale forcefully at the moment of impact, or possibly *kiai* (battle cry). In rushing forward, bring the back leg sharply through to the front, thereby catapulting the entire body powerfully forward. In this punch, the body remains erect and the shoulders are not thrust forward (see Illus. 24). In the *Shotokan* method, the back leg passes close by the forward leg in a slight semicircle and is set down towards the outside. In the *Wado-ryu* system, it moves straight forward.

Special Training for Oi-tsuki (Illus. 25 and 26)

An excellent exercise for the fist punch is to practice with bicycle innertubes. Tie three innertubes together. Grasp the end of one innertube with the punching hand. In the starting position *(gedangamae)*, hold out the innertube loosely straight while the other end is fastened down at hip-height, or held by a comrade. Now execute *oi-tsuki*. Because of the powerful tension in the bicycle innertubes, you are forced to go forward correctly, to have a sure stance, and to breathe correctly. Only in this way can the application of the force of the entire body be so directed as to overcome the pulling power of the innertubes. Practice this 50 times with each side of the body. Exhale forcefully with each application of force.

Illus. 25   **Illus. 26**

Gyaku-tsuki, the reverse punch, from zenkutsu-dachi (Illus. 27 to 33)

Thrust the left leg forward but punch with the right fist, hence, "reverse" punch. This punch is made very powerful by bringing the back leg through to the front and twisting in the hips very sharply (Illus. 27 to 29). In moving forward, keep well

Illus. 27   Illus. 28   Illus. 29

Illus. 30 Illus. 31 Illus. 32

down; draw the forward-moving leg close to the standing leg in passing (Illus. 30 and 31) and set it down in an outward arc to the front, with the ball of the foot foremost. Then, upon settling the ball of the foot, immediately throw the body forward by means of the powerful bringing through to the front of the back leg. In doing this, turn the hips sharply inwards and at the last moment of this turning movement, shoot the punching fist powerfully forward so that the power and speed of the turning hips can be transmitted entirely to the punching fist (Illus. 32). Attack the solar plexus or the face.

Illus. 33

Special Training for Gyaku-tsuki (Illus. 34 to 37)

Another excellent exercise for the fist punch is punching while holding small dumbbells. Here, too, punch 50 times with full strength (Illus. 34 and 35).

Illus. 34   Illus. 35   Illus. 36

Illus. 37

Afterwards, always do a few fist punches without the dumbbells. (Illus. 36 shows the movement for the bicycle innertube training for *gyaku-tsuki*.) In addition, to harden the fists' punching surfaces, practice with the *makiwara* (Illus. 37).

Illus. 38

Illus. 39

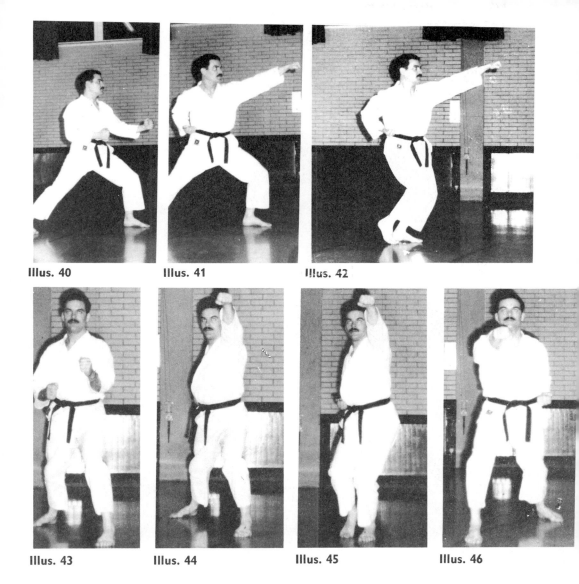

Illus. 40   Illus. 41   Illus. 42

Illus. 43   Illus. 44   Illus. 45   Illus. 46

Kizami-tsuki/Oi-tsuki (Illus. 38 to 46)

From the starting stance (Illus. 38), punch with *kizami-tsuki* towards the face. (*Kizami-tsuki* is a punch without a focal point; in punching, the shoulder is thrust forward, the hips turned away.) Immediately after the punching arm is fully extended (Illus. 39), bring the back leg forward without a pause (Illus. 40) and go

29

forward with *oi-tsuki* (Illus. 41 and 42). (Illus. 43 to 46 show this combination from the front.) The hip, which in *kizami-tsuki* is turned away, can in the following *oi-tsuki* be thrown forward and this way be placed again in a straight position.

In executing *kizami-tsuki*, set the front leg forward with a gliding step and punch so close to the opponent's face that he is sufficiently menaced.

Kizami-tsuki/Gyaku-tsuki (Illus. 47 to 54)

This combination is the most frequently used in fighting practice. Practice it left and right, mainly as in basic school. Then practice it in a free stance and with a snap-back of the punching fist.

From the starting stance (Illus. 47), spring with lightning speed on the opponent with *kizami-tsuki*, hurling the body forward from the *hara* (Illus. 48 to 49). Upon landing, immediately punch with *gyaku-tsuki* towards the solar plexus, applying force *(kime)* with full emphasis *(kiai)* (Illus. 50). Thus, the body is thrown directly

Illus. 49   **Illus. 50**

Illus. 51　　　　**Illus. 52**　　　　**Illus. 53**　　　　**Illus. 54**

Illus. 55

forward from the *hara*, finding its climax in powerful *gyaku-tsuki*. Everything is executed simultaneously—in a single, swift forward movement. Illus. 51 to 54 and Illus. 55 show the basic school execution of *kizami-tsuki*.

To get a better sense of these direct fighting combinations, picture the action of a rubber band that is stretched and then released. You can also compare the karate attack with the movement of a cat that lies in wait and then attacks its quarry: Wait watchfully in a low, ducked position, then spring softly and swiftly upon your target (movement impulse), grabbing it upon landing with your full strength (power impulse or *kime*). In the *kizami-tsuki/gyaku-tsuki* combination, therefore, the focal point or power impulse lies in *gyaku-tsuki*.

31

Illus. 56   **Illus. 57**   **Illus. 58**   **Illus. 59**

Leg Techniques (Keri)

Force is also transmitted to the target by means of leg movements. In all leg techniques, the snapping movement is placed mainly in the knee joint. First, the bended knee is snapped upwards, then the foot snaps out to the target and is snapped back again without interruption. At the same time, the hips are thrust sharply in the direction of the foot technique. Done this way, the technique is more a straight, powerful kick *(keri-ke-komi)* which has its principal source in the snapping movement of the knee and is outwardly directed *(keri-keage)*.

As a rule, kicking at longer distances is done with *ke-komi* as throwing the hips into the kick lengthens its reach. For shorter distances, the foot is lifted rapidly upwards with *keage (age* = lift).

Mae-geri, the frontal kick (Illus. 56 to 61)

Bring the knee sharply upwards and without interrupting the movement, thrust the foot towards the target and again spring it back (Illus. 56 to 59 is one act). Not until then is the foot set down lightly and noiselessly (Illus. 60).

In executing this technique, the upper part of the thighs should maintain contact with each other as long as possible and the weight-bearing leg and the knee of the kicking leg should point forward. The kick should be aimed at the opponent's midsection, so that all muscles, particularly those of the lower abdomen *(hara)*, can be concentrated in the technique. Kick with the ball of the foot. This way, injury is avoided as the toes are bent upwards and strengthen the ankle (see also Illus. 61).

Illus. 60   Illus. 61

The center of gravity of the body must be kept low. Do not straighten, but *bend* the weight-bearing leg. Keep your balance!

Mawashi-geri, the roundhouse kick (Illus. 62 to 66)

Bring the knee up to a horizontal position and kick forward without interruption. Attack from the side with the ball of the foot or the instep. In this, the weight-

Illus. 62   Illus. 63   Illus. 64

Illus. 65   **Illus. 66**

bearing leg must be turned 45° (at the most 90°) otherwise; the power cannot be concentrated in the direction of attack.

Yoko-geri, the side kick or Sokuto (edge of the foot) (Illus. 67 to 72)

Here the edge of the foot near the heel is brought into play as a weapon. Lift the knee up (Illus. 67 and 68), then kick the obliquely held foot (as much as possible, the sole of the foot must always be kept parallel to the floor) towards the target with a sharp thrust of the hips *(yoko-geri-ke-komi*, Illus. 69) or move it sharply upwards from the knee joint (*yoko-geri-keage*, Illus. 72). Bring the knee back to its lifted position, then set it down forward to *yoko-geri* with the other foot (Illus. 70 and 71).

Ushiro-geri, the kick to the rear (Illus. 73 to 76)

Glance over the shoulder towards the target on the side of the kicking leg (Illus. 73). Then, raise the knee and without interruption, kick directly backwards towards the target (Illus. 74 to 76). The upper part of the thighs must maintain contact with each other as long as possible. The leg must be fully stretched out. Strike with the heel. Finally, the leg is immediately drawn back to the raised-knee position shown in Illus. 74, then set down.

Important Principles for All Foot Techniques

1. Bring the knee sharply upwards; then, without interruption of the movement, shoot the leg towards the target and immediately snap it back again.

34

Illus. 67   Illus. 68   Illus. 69

Illus. 70   Illus. 71   Illus. 72

2. Bend the weight-bearing leg well and press the sole of the foot firmly against the floor so that you can ward off the recoil when the foot strikes the target.

3. Also, the leg techniques must be brought to rest precisely. You must be able to strike out at full strength with millimeter-precision.

4. In this, the correct tension (breathing) in the lower abdomen *(hara)* helps. The hips especially are not bent in foot techniques. If you bend your hips, you cannot transfer the force from the lower abdomen to the foot technique. The technique is thus weakened, for it also receives its decisive force from the *hara*, in connection with correct breathing.

Illus. 73   Illus. 74   Illus. 75

Illus. 76

Practice Methods

Here are more special forms and practice methods for leg techniques.

1. Some forms of *Ushiro-geri*. *Ushiro-geri* is a good fighting technique. The danger of injury is small and it is difficult to ward off when executed swiftly and forcefully.

(a) *Ushiro-geri* from the forward turn (Illus. 77 to 80)

Bring the knee up sharply, turn on the bent weight-bearing leg and throw the hips forcibly in the direction of the kick. In doing this, do not let your opponent out of your sight. With this technique, you can keep the opponent in reach of your attack—from directly in front to the right of you (a quarter-circle).

Illus. 77

Illus. 78

Illus. 79

Illus. 80

Illus. 81

Illus. 82

Illus. 83

(b) *Ushiro-geri* from the back turn (Illus. 81 to 83)

Place the ball of the forward foot at a right angle to the opponent (Illus. 81). Now, quickly turn your back to the opponent. This must take place as quickly as possible, for here lies the danger-point in this technique: the opponent is briefly lost from your field of view. Immediately glance over the right shoulder towards the opponent (Illus. 82) and making use of the force developed in turning, kick in a straight line directly towards him (Illus. 83). In this way of using *ushiro-geri*, make sure that the upper parts of the thighs maintain contact for as long as possible, so that the kick strikes the target in a straight line and does not develop into a wide-ranging arc because of the turning. Otherwise, it is not possible to transmit the force from the *hara* into the kick. Moreover, the technique is thus slowed down, cannot be arrested (no focal point), and throws you off balance.

38

With this form of *ushiro-geri*, you can reach an opponent who stands either directly in front or to the left of you (quarter-circle arc). The moment in which you do not have him in sight is so brief that he will have considerable difficulty in reaching the "blind spot" behind your back. Nevertheless, use this technique with caution and maximum alertness.

(c) *Ushiro-geri* from pursuit (Illus. 84 to 86)

An opponent who retreats before your attack can be easily reached with the following use of *ushiro-geri*:

From the right-foot-forward stance (Illus. 84), the left leg, crossed behind, is brought far forward (Illus. 85). The ball of the foot is thus lightly planted. Pass the bodyweight over upon the left leg and at the same time kick to the right with *ushiro-geri*, making use of the impetus of the forward movement (Illus. 86). Thus, the attack involves the full employment of the body, making it powerful and very difficult to ward off.

Illus. 84

Illus. 85

Illus. 86

Illus. 87   Illus. 88

Illus. 89   Illus. 90

2. Practice Form for *Mae—Yoko* and *Ushiro-geri* in Combination (Illus. 87 to 93) Start from the right forward stance. First, move forward with *mae-geri* left (Illus. 87). Immediately after this first step, your partner takes a step backwards so that you can go no farther forward with *mae-geri* right (Illus. 88). Your partner again takes a step backwards and you pursue with *yoko-geri* left (Illus. 89). Again, set the kicking leg down in front while your partner goes back another step; then kick right with *yoko-geri* (Illus. 90). Now put the kicking leg down in front at a right angle to your partner (Illus. 91). Quickly turn around on the balls of the feet and kick with *ushiro-geri* from the back turn (Illus. 91 and Illus. 92). To conclude, *mae-geri* right

Illus. 91

Illus. 92

Illus. 93

(Illus. 93). With each foot technique, your partner takes another step backwards. Now it is your partner's turn. When you have arrived at the starting position, practice it once more, only this time, begin with a right *mae-geri*. This way, you can practice foot techniques left and right while focussing on a target that is right before your eyes.

Illus. 95

Illus. 94

3. A Practice Form for *Mae-geri* (Illus. 94 and 95)

The class stands in a circle (or in a row) in left-foot-forward stance. Each one counts to ten, while doing *mae-geri* (at least five men doing 50 kicks; if time allows, increase to ten men doing 100 kicks). Afterwards, practice with the other foot.

4. A Practice Form for *Mawashi-geri* (Illus. 96 to 100)

Stand in two opposite rows (Illus. 96 and 97). The man at the right end of the line counts, "One!" and every karateka in the same row kicks with *mawashi-geri* towards the solar plexus of his partner (Illus. 98 and 100). Then, the man on the

Illus. 96

Illus. 97

Illus. 98

Illus. 99

Illus. 100

right end of the opposite row calls out loudly, "Two!" and all the kareteka in this row kick their turn of *mawashi-geri* (Illus. 99). After some time, switch: those who had the right-foot-forward stance take on the left-foot-forward stance and vice versa.

5. Target Practice for *Mae-geri* and *Yoko-geri* (Illus. 101 to 102)

Your partner stands in *zenkutsu-dachi* right. Grab his right sleeve and kick ten times under his chin with the ball of the foot. Now it is his turn. Finally, practice left.

For *yoko-geri*, your partner must stand in *kiba-dachi*. Let your foot snap upwards with *yoko-geri keage*, so that its edge comes to rest under his chin. Strike here with extreme precision, powerfully and precisely restrained. Make sure that your techniques with *kime* (focal point) are struck to the target point with millimeter-precision.

Illus. 102

Illus. 101

Defence Techniques (Uke)

Since karate was originally an art of war, its defence techniques have been highly developed. It is said that the true art of karate is to begin and end with a defence. It follows from this that karate is not, in essence, an attack weapon.

Most karate defences are defences with a "focal point" *(kime)*; that is, in the short moment of contact, the power of the entire body is concentrated in the point of impact and then immediately dissipates again as in attack techniques. The

44

advantage of this defence with a focal point is that it submits the attacker to such pain, on account of the shock effect, that he refrains from further attack. During a defence with a focal point, it is advisable not to fall out of balance and to be immediately ready to execute the next technique—either attack or further defence.

Important Principles of Defence

1. Try to turn the attacker's force to your own advantage.
2. Always keep your balance.
3. Keep your mind on the fact that the decisive force must lie in counterattack. For this reason, do not put too much emphasis on defence, but while defending, think ahead of the counterattack you will execute in conclusion.
4. Be careful that you do not expose any weak points to your attacker. Remember that in defence, the decisive power comes from the hips (hara). At the moment of defensive action, they are turned away most energetically, strengthening the opposing force of the defence and making the surfaces exposed to the opponent's attack smaller. Immediately following the defensive action, the powerful turning back of the hips can be brought into action for the counterattack.

The defence must strike the attacking arm or the attacking leg while it is still in motion. Simultaneously with the defence, move your body out of the danger zone, possibly by as little as turning the hips (see *soto-ude-uke*, page 47 and *gedan-barai*, page 49). This way, and by not blocking the entire, oncoming energy and "dissipating" it in the defensive arm (resulting in pain or injury), the force is merely turned aside into empty space and you are ready, with all your strength and without delay, for the counterattack. For this reason, move your body in such a way that you can immediately execute a counterattack. (See Point 1 and Point 3.) Do not simply move forward in defensive action, but in more of a sliding manner (forward or backwards).

The Upwards Block (Age-uke or Jodan-uke)

The attacking arm is fended off with the outer side of the forearm (Illus. 103 to 106).

Avoid the following mistakes:

1. Do not lift the shoulder of the defending arm. That will prevent the power from the lower abdomen (hara) from strengthening the blocking move with the side muscles of the trunk.
2. The elbow must not be higher than the hand. Otherwise, the defence is enormously weakened.
3. The elbow of the defensive arm must not stand out from the side of the body.

Illus. 103   Illus. 104   Illus. 105   Illus. 106

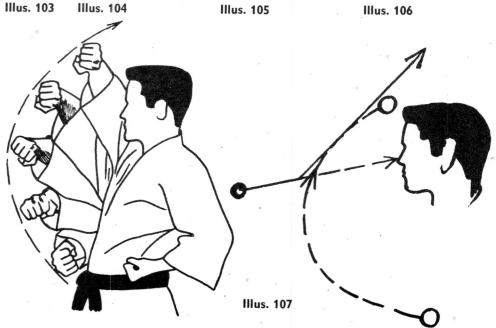

Illus. 107

Otherwise, you will not succeed in concentrating the full power of your body in the point of impact (see Illus. 106).

Seen from the side, the defending forearm describes an ascending arc, so that the power of the attacking arm is not "nullified" but simply turned aside (Illus. 107). So for your defence, you do not need much force because the movement of the attacking arm is not stopped but continued and your counterattack takes place while his attacking arm is still in movement.

(Chudan) Soto-ude-uke, Defence with the Outer (soto) Side of the Forearm (Illus. 108-113)

In *Wado-ryu*, this defence is called *uchi-ude-uke*, because the defensive movement travels from the outside towards the inside *(= uchi)* (Illus. 108 to 111 and 113). The force of the defence comes mainly from the hips. The fist of the defending arm here also completely turns and rests exactly opposite the shoulder of the other arm (Illus. 112).

Blocking is done with the fleshy part of the forearm near the elbow (Illus. 112). Hit the attacking arm as far forward towards the wrist as possible, thus throwing the attacker off balance by means of his own force. Here the defending arm goes along

Illus. 108

Illus. 109

Illus. 110

Illus. 111

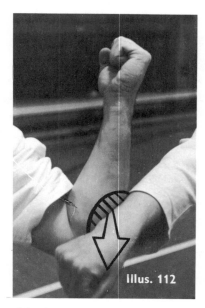

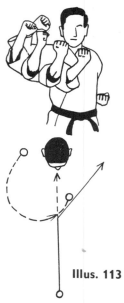

Illus. 112

Illus. 113

with the attacking arm in the direction of attack, thus, an elegant defence is executed (Illus. 112 and Illus. 113).

Illus. 114

Illus. 115

Illus. 116

Uchi-ude-uke, Defence with the Inner (uchi) Side of the Forearm (Illus. 114–116)

In *Wado-ryu*, this defence is called *soto-ude-uke*, because the defensive movement travels from the inside towards the outside *(soto)*. With the elbow as the center of the turning movement, snap the forearm outwards and strengthen it by turning the hips towards the opposing force. With this manoeuvre, defence cannot be as "soft" as in the use of *age-uke* or *soto-ude-uke*, but the arm is caused to rebound to the side against the direction of the attack. Here, also, the fist is turned in the final position.

Gedan-barai, the Downwards Block with the Forearm (Illus. 117–122)

This defence is directed particularly against a leg attack. It is also struck with the elbow as the center of rotation. Turning the hips strengthens the manoeuvre through the opposing force of the defence. This defence shunts aside the mass of the attacking member in a way similar to *uchi-ude-uke*. In free-style fighting, this defence can also be so executed (in connection with evasion) that it does not stop the attacking force dead but causes it to pass on. (See fighting combinations on page 69.)

Illus. 117   **Illus. 118**

Illus. 120

Illus. 121

Illus. 122

Shuto–uke, Defence with the Edge of the Hand (Illus. 123–129)

The attacking arm is struck off to the side with the edge of the hand. In *Wado-ryu*, the defence is directed against attack to the *jodan* level (Illus. 123 to 127). In *Shotokan* style, the *chudan* defence is executed (Illus. 128 and Illus. 129).

Illus. 123

Illus. 124

Illus. 125

Illus. 126

Illus. 127

Illus. 128

Illus. 129

In principle, *shuto-uke* works similarly to the two previously described arm techniques, *gedan-barai* and *uchi-ude-uke*. With the elbow as a turning point, the attacking member is shunted off to the side. This defence, however, is not as elegant as *age-uke* and *soto-ude-uke*. Here, the two forces—attack and defence—are almost directly opposed to each other. In contrast, the defensive movement in *age-uke* and *soto-ude-uke* adapts itself to the direction of the attack, easily and smartly deflecting it.

In all three, *uchi-ude-uke, gedan-barai* and *shuto-uke*, the attacking force is stronger than the defensive force. Thus, it is possible that the attack might pass through the defence, since the defensive movement is directed against the movement of attack (Illus. 130). To offset this possibility, one must rely on the most important movement in karate—the movement of the hips *(hara)* from which every movement receives its degree and direction of force.

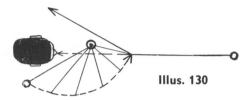

Illus. 130

Earlier on, we learned that the consequence of turning the hips away is the most important factor in defence:

1. The surfaces exposed to the opponent become smaller.

2. For the counterattack, immediately following the defence, you can turn the hips sharply and powerfully back as they were before. The counterattack obtains its decisive force from this turning of the hips.

3. By means of the sharp turning away of the hips, the opposing force in the defending arm is strengthened.

However, why is turning the hips so important in *uchi-ude-uke, gedan-barai* and *shuto-uke*, especially when the attack is so powerful it cannot be struck aside with the defending arm? Let the hips (and with them the entire body) remain motionless and try to defend only with the limbs. In such a case, a stronger attack passes right through, since force is ranged against force. However, turn the hips (and with them the body) sharply away and at the same time crouch from the powerful attack—the blow does not touch you, even when you succeed only in striking the attacking limb no more than a centimetre aside. (Illus. 131 and 132 show *gedan-barai*; Illus. 133 and 134 *uchi-ude-uke*.) In practice, naturally, this crouching of one's own body away from attack and the shunting aside of the force of the attacking member are executed simultaneously.

It can never be over-emphasized that the movements in true karate must always be movements of the entire body, originating from the hips, and not merely movements of the arms and legs. This way, an "economical" defence is made possible in *uchi-ude-uke*, *gedan-barai*, and *shuto-uke*, actions in which the attacking movement is not stopped dead or "nullified" (with danger of injury), but in which you crouch away out of the direction of attack without risk that your defence may be "broken through" by a very powerful attack. The term "breakthrough" is suitable for something that is firm and rigid. During a defensive play, however, the body should never be motionless and rigid. The defence should always consist much more of arm and body movements.

Illus. 131

Illus. 132

Illus. 133

Illus. 134

Practice Forms for Defence Techniques

Illustrations 135 to 140 present an extremely outstanding form of practice for defences in connection with counterattack. In this, turning the hips in defence and counterattack is especially developed. Moreover, defence becomes a positive reflex. Through this practice form you can sharpen the defence techniques which you are most frequently called upon to use: *age-uke*, *soto-ude-uke* and *gedan-barai*.

Continuously punched and defended in turn are the upper trunk, the middle trunk, the lower trunk, and immediately again the upper trunk, etc.

Illus. 135

Illus. 136

Illus. 137

Illus. 138

Illus. 139

Illus. 140

Illus. 141

Illus. 142

Illus. 143

Illus. 144

Illus. 145

Here are two more practice forms for pure defence:

1. Stand with your back to a wall. Your partner attacks with *jodan-tsuki* in irregular order and wherever you present an opening at the time. In defence, you must work from the hips, duck down, turn away, and so on. This practice is also a good reaction training. The same thing may be said for the next practice, in which you must indeed defend yourself against all kinds of attacks *(tsuki* and *keri)* (Illus. 141 to 145).

2. Stand in a very low and tensed position, one that would not be practical for fighting but strengthens your muscles and tendons. Your feet must remain always on the same spot. Your partner attacks with *tsuki* or *keri*. Here, as in the foregoing practice, only limited evasion with the body is possible, i.e., by a shifting of the bodyweight from the hips. Body turns from the hips are especially good practice for the development of positive reflexes in defence in connection with shifting the weight (Illus. 146 to 150).

Illus. 146

Illus. 147

Illus. 148

Illus. 149 **Illus. 150**

Basic Techniques in Combination

Before we come to the principles and techniques of free-style fighting, I must describe still another combination of basic techniques which are required in the karate examination program and have already, in hindsight, been added to free-style contests. These combinations have, for this reason, already been presented in free form.

1. Mae-geri/Gyaku-tsuki (Illus. 151–154)

This combination is required for the 5th *kyu* degree (yellow belt). The combinations must be introduced in a fluent manner as a unity. From the starting position (Illus. 151), kick out powerfully with *mae-geri* (Illus. 152). In doing so, throw your body forward from the *hara*, along with the kick and land with a powerful *gyaku-tsuki* (Illus. 153 and 154).

Illus. 151 **Illus. 152** **Illus. 153** **Illus. 154**

57

2. Mae-geri/Jodan-chudan Rentsuki (Illus. 155–158)

Illus. 155

Illus. 156

Illus. 157

Illus. 158

3. Yoko-geri/Uraken/Gyaku-tsuki (Illus. 159-165)

Illus. 159

Illus. 160

Illus. 161

Illus. 162

Illus. 163

Illus. 164

Illus. 165

4. Mawashi-geri/Ushiro-geri/Uraken (Jodan)/Gyaku-tsuki (Chudan)

In utilizing the turning movement of the hips in *mawashi-geri*, set the kicking leg down and turn (Illus. 166 to 169), continuing immediately into *ushiro-geri* (Illus. 170). When your body stands sideways to the opponent after a foot technique *(yoko-geri, mawashi-geri,* or *ushiro-geri),* always pursue with *uraken/gyaku-tsuki* (Illus. 171 to 173). Both techniques quickly follow each other after the turning in of the hips. *Uraken* to the opponent's face or knock aside his covering hand towards either the inside or the outside.

Illus. 166

Illus. 167

Illus. 168

Illus. 169

Illus. 170

Illus. 171 **Illus. 172** **Illus. 173**

II. A Summary of Considerations on Basic Techniques

The world-renowned Japanese karate master, Hirokazu Kanazawa, 5th Dan, once said, "There are three ways to become a good karateka: 1. Basic Training; 2. Basic Training; 3. Basic Training."

Needless to say, this does not mean going without fighting training and especially not without the *kata*. When asked whether he had always prepared himself for championship matches, Kanazawa answered, "In the days before the tournament, I trained especially hard in basic techniques." In other words, the key to success is the constant strengthening of the karateka's grasp of the basic techniques! Therefore, it would be useful to review some fundamental principles of karate.

The most important source of power for all movements of the entire body lies in the body's center of gravity in the region of the hips, more specifically, in the lower abdomen or the *hara*. It is from the *hara* that movements in karate originate and receive dimension and direction.

The muscles of the abdominal region are strong but slow, while the muscles of the extremities are weak but fast. Therefore, in karate, the hip region moves first, then the limbs. This roots the limbs to the strong abdominal region. Since every technique receives its decisive power from the *hara*, there must exist a direct connection with the *hara* at the moment of impact. In this short moment, this connection must be without any soft spots so that the power of the *hara* can be transmitted to the point of impact, the high point of tension. Your *hara* can work powerfully only when you do not break in the abdominal region. Otherwise, this potent source of power becomes closed to you and your karate consists only of swift but weak movements of the limbs as the powerful "middle" is lacking! For this reason, keep the body absolutely erect in all techniques! Only in this way can you give strength to the middle of the body and transmit it to the limbs.

To understand this principle better, let us examine its application in the fist punch.

Basically, the punching arm must be completely outstretched. The connection with the powerful muscles of the lower body takes place mainly through the breast muscles. This tension of the side breast muscles is extremely important to all arm techniques including defence and striking techniques. Therefore, under no condition must the shoulder be lifted. Lifting the shoulder makes it impossible to tense these side muscles and leads to the enormous weakening of the technique.

The returning fist must be withdrawn completely and the elbow must be pressed in toward the spine. Through this, the other half of the body is brought under tension. Otherwise, with a one-sided tension, your technique is not so effective. Moreover, you weaken quite considerably your own stability and a light blow forward with the open hand against the punching fist is all that is needed to knock you off balance.

Another point to remember is that direct connections exist between many techniques. (See the basic textbook.) Seek out and learn to recognize such interdependencies. Both *oi-tsuki* and *mae-geri*, for example, use the direct hurling forward of the body from the *hara*.

Common to both *gyaku-tsuki* and *mawashi-geri* is the sharp twisting of the hips. Here can be seen with special clarity the correctness of the basic principles, "movement of the hips first, then movement of the extremities." A similar connection also exists between the movements in *uchi-ude-uke* and those of *yoko-geri*. The turning or twisting of the hips is also the most important movement in defence technique. In defence techniques, twisting the hips sharply away produces a strengthened opposing force that is transmitted to the defending arm. (See also "Counter Techniques," "Free-Style Fighting"; also "Defence Techniques.")

Sensei Kanazawa holds that in karate, even a man of 70 years is still hale and hearty and strikes just as fast and hard as a young man. (See Illus. 4, where Gichin Funakoshi, the founder of karate, demonstrates karate techniques at the age of 88.) Kanazawa explains: "All of karate goes out from the lower abdomen *(hara)*. In old age, the muscles of the face and of the extremities can indeed become flabbier, but the muscles of the lower abdomen remain strong." Grasp this correct understanding firmly and practice the basic techniques tirelessly in every training session. This is the key to success.

III. Free-Style Fighting

In its original form, karate is a method of fighting involving two opponents. Even today, this free style of fighting still represents the highest form of karate. The demands of stopping the attack just before body contact is made require and develop extreme body-control and self-discipline. This level is reserved only for those karateka who have reached this stage by means of intensive practice in the basic techniques. This way, it is possible to remove danger from the contests.

It is worthwhile to remember that in a karate contest it is made especially clear that neither victory nor defeat is the principal goal, rather victory over oneself (physically and mentally). Only he who has his body and mind under complete control has a chance of winning. Character training thus stands in first place and victory over others, second. Only those who recognize this true essence of karate will be able to learn karate correctly.

The way to free-style fighting *(jiyu-kumite)* starts from learning single techniques in basic training *(kihon)*. This is followed by simple partner practice in *ippon* and *sanbon-kumite*, the half-free partner contest *(jiyu-ippon-kumite)*, then culminates in the highest level of free fighting between two karateka who have passed all the way through the long training in strength, precision and accuracy.

This chapter shows you techniques for free-style fighting which are of key importance to advanced students. The beginner, too, can practice these free-style fighting techniques with great profit but must take care not to fall into the mistake of thereby neglecting the basic techniques. In fact, even an advanced student should place great value on the practice of basic techniques in *kihon*.*

Basic Principles of Free-Style Fighting

1. The Fighting Stance

Each can choose the fighting stance best suited to him. In every case, however, avoid tense, cramped positions. Only from a relaxed posture and a relaxed mental state can you react with lightning speed. In Illus. 174, Master Toyama demonstrates a very beautiful fighting stance, which shows quite clearly, by means of an uncramped and erect posture, the "inner preparedness." Observe how the

---

*NOTE: For further information on *ippon-* and *sanbon-kumite*, as well as on *kihon* and *jiyu-ippon-kumite*, see "Karate: Basic Principles."

Illus. 174

posture is concentrated in the *hara* and how he stands loosely, yet filled with "inner preparedness" in the middle of the right side of the body.

2. Distance from Opponent

Choose a distance far enough apart that you are always beyond the reach of your opponent. However, that goes only for the passive part of the fight. In order to gain a point, you must come within arm's length or leg's length of your opponent.

If you are smaller than your opponent, run up close to him so that he cannot find enough room for his longer arms and legs. You, on the other hand, then gain the correct distance for your techniques. If you are bigger than your opponent, you must keep him at a distance so that you will always have the correct attack distance for your longer arms and legs. You can measure your distance from your opponent in such a way that you can stand too near him for his foot techniques to be effective and yet not be in reach of his arm techniques. From such a position, you can have freedom of action. This ploy is especially effective if you have fist techniques.

If in the course of the fight the distance apart becomes so small that you are in reach of his fist punches (Illus. 175), you must be the one to attack immediately and

without hesitation. Otherwise, a lightning-fast punching attack (or possibly a double-punch *jodan-chudan*) will, in this case, be very difficult to ward off (Illus. 176).

3. Guard

If the distance to your opponent is too great, cover the lower part of your body since it will be the target of your opponent's first attacks which will consist of foot techniques (Illus. 177). If the distance becomes less, your guard should go up along your body as now arm techniques are to be expected from your opponent (Illus. 178). Keep your arms bent. If your opponent holds his arms outstretched (Illus.

Illus. 177   Illus. 178

Illus. 179   Illus. 180

179), attack immediately. In order to be able to react (in defence or counterattack), he must, of course, first bend his arms and in this period of time your attack can penetrate (Illus. 180).

4. Movement

Choose a pace that is different from that of your opponent. For example, if your opponent hardly moves and stands well guarded in a strong stance, keep moving and try to make him move about so that you can attack. However, if your opponent attacks you on swift, running legs, take a low stance to increase your strength. Block any attack of your opponent and immediately execute a counterattack.

To understand these ideas on movement correctly, it is important to pay attention to the movement of the mind, in addition to the movement of the body. If you yourself persist in a strong, motionless position, your mind must be awake and in motion. If in fighting you move around quickly, your mind, on the other hand, must remain calm. Otherwise, you attack too hurriedly, nervously, and grasp the changing combat situations too late. Your mind must be ready, quiet and calm as water in a pool—always ready to flow to wherever it is needed.

To sum up, in order to measure up to all your opponents, you must be master of all paces. Fight quickly and with movement against a strong, motionless opponent; stand strong and well guarded against an opponent who moves around. During a fight, change the pace as often as possible. Attack your opponent with several techniques and make him move around, or let him come near you and then counter his attack. Also, keep in mind that in attacking, make not only one attack but always a series of attacks (combinations). In defence, do not always retreat defensively. After the second or third parry, stand firm and counter immediately. It is even better to glide sideways out of the line of attack, especially after the opponent's second or third attempt when he attacks in succession, and, at the same time or immediately following, to execute a counterattack. Remember above all to keep your hips in movement and thereby cause your opponent's attack to be wasted.

5. The Fighting Method

If your opponent is tall, he fights in a high, frontal stance with very good guard against attack from the front. This is often the fighting method of tall karateka. They march immediately upon you and parry quite easily with their strong frontal guard every doubtfully executed "stopping attempt" you may resist with. Here, do not fall into the error of becoming involved in a "retreat." Remember that you are very strong in a low, motionless stance. Assume this stance, block your opponent's attack and counter immediately. With an erect body you can have a lower center of gravity than your opponent. This makes you potentially stronger and gives you the advantage. Therefore, go ahead on your own account and attack, always from the low stance which, however, should remain relaxed even in the midst of your attack movements. Another possibility is always to move sideways towards your opponent and to attack from the side. With his frontal fighting method, he is not accustomed to this approach and it confuses him. Thus, you can create gaps in his cover and turn them to your own good account.

IV. Combination Techniques

In karate contests *(jiyu-kumite)*, you always look for or try to bring about openings in your opponent's defences and, with lightning speed, exploit them to your advantage. Since your opponent is also a karateka, you must indeed be above average in speed in order to come through with a direct attack. As in judo fighting, in which a good judoka also seldom attacks directly but always works with combinations, a karateka should not attack only once but always in a series of attacks, unless he is very fast and can therefore make direct use of every opening his opponent inadvertently offers. The karateka, therefore, should concern himself with combination techniques to be successful in fighting.

The following are the possibilities for combinations of karate techniques:

1. *Tsuki-tsuki (-keri)*
2. *Tsuki-keri (-tsuki)*
3. *Keri-keri (-tsuki)*
4. *Keri-tsuki (-tsuki)*

In practicing a series of attacks, accustom yourself to always following the foot techniques with one or several fist punches. Avoid working only with foot techniques—a mistake beginners only too easily fall into.

Naturally, combinations of three or four techniques are also possible. It is very much to your advantage if you master at least one combination out of each of these groups.

Combination Hand Techniques

In karate contests, make use of the fist punch *(tsuki)* most of all. It is the fastest and most direct technique, which you can shoot out without "telegraphing." The fist punch is among the principal weapons in karate fighting and should not be neglected. As an advanced student, practice it tirelessly, even setting aside a few minutes for it at home. This way, you can make it continually faster and more powerful.

Jodan kizami-tsuki/Gyaku-tsuki (Illus. 181 to 185)

Jodan kizami-tsuki is a fist punch to the upper trunk without a focal point, the only purpose of which is to divert the opponent's attention and possibly drive his guard upwards to create an opening for a real attack.

Do not attack frontally with *jodan kizami-tsuki* (Illus. 181). Otherwise you will probably run right into your opponent's straight left. Attack sideways and in doing so fend his forward guard arm somewhat inwards with your punching arm (Illus. 182). In this way, you run no danger of being countered by him. With lightning

Illus. 181

Illus. 182

Illus. 183

Illus. 184

Illus. 185

speed, place your right forward leg to the side and then attack *chudan* with a left *gyaku-tsuki* (Illus. 183). The same combination which is required in the 6th *kyu* grade (white belt), is, of course, possible the other way around—left forward leg, right *gyaku-tsuki*. However, you can punch better with *kizami-tsuki* from the outside over the opponent's forward guarding arm, as this brings you closer to his back side (Illus. 184). Here then, as a second technique, *gyaku-tsuki* right is possible or, if you are closer to the opponent, *shuto-uchi* to the kidneys (Illus. 185), or *mawashi-tsuki* to the back of the head or nape.

Uraken-uchi/Gyaku-tsuki (Illus. 186 to 188)

This too is a combination *jodan/chudan*. Glide forward and strike sideways with *uraken* (Illus. 187) or downwards from above (Illus. 186), then immediately place the forward leg to the side with *gyaku-tsuki chudan* (Illus. 188). It is important not only to feint above and to attack below while your body remains virtually motionless, but also to "carry your body along" by changing the position of the legs to shift the weight. This makes the actual attack technique more effective. Moreover, the opponent is kept worried by the fact that in this combination, your body moves constantly.

These are only two examples of the first group of combination possibilities. It is, of course, also possible to attack the other way around—first *chudan*, then make use of the openings that are thereby created in the opponent's cover.

Illus. 186

Illus. 187

Illus. 188

Combination Arm and Foot Techniques

In this set of combinations, feinting is mostly done above, and the opening, which is thereby created below, is taken advantage of with a foot technique.

Kizami-tsuki/Mae-geri (Illus. 189 to 192)

Here again, a movement from the forward hurling of the body with *kizami-tsuki*

Illus. 189

Illus. 190

Illus. 191

Illus. 192

(Illus. 189 to 191), culminates powerfully in *mae-geri* (Illus. 192). The punching fist remains forward to confuse the opponent.

Gyaku-tsuki/Mae-geri (Illus. 193 and 194)

Immediately after feinting with the fist towards the opponent's face (Illus. 193), thrust the foot (on the same side of the body) swiftly forward in *mae-geri* (Illus. 194).

Illus. 193

Illus. 194

Illus. 195   Illus. 196

Kizami-tsuki/Mawashi-geri (Illus. 195 and 196)

Kizami-tsuki from the outside (Illus. 195) followed by a roundhouse kick (Illus. 196).

Combination Foot Techniques

Mae-(or yoko)geri/Ushiro-geri (Illus. 197 and 198)

After the first kick in *ushiro-geri*, depending on how far and in which direction the opponent retreats, follow through from the forward turn or the reverse turn, or from a position of pursuit (see *ushiro-geri* on page 34).

Illus. 197   Illus. 198

Yoko-geri/Mawashi-geri (Illus. 199 and 200)

In this combination, the power of the hip turning can be thrown beautifully into the second technique.

Illus. 199

Illus. 200

Mawashi-geri/Mawashi-geri (Illus. 201 and 202)

Deliver continuous attacks with *mawashi-geri* if the opponent gives ground.

Illus. 201

Illus. 202

Combination Foot and Arm Technique

The openings created by means of a foot attack are taken advantage of with *tsuki*. After a foot attack, you are usually too far from the opponent for a following fist attack. Moreover, he usually moves backwards (retreats). (See Illus. 203.) Therefore, you must bridge a longer distance than is possible with the mere setting of the kicking foot down in its foremost position. Here, the stored tension in the bent, weight-supporting leg helps (Illus. 204). By it, you can catapult yourself far forward (Illus. 205 and Illus. 206). In this action, pull the back leg along (a gliding step) and immediately upon placing the feet, deliver a punch (Illus. 207) in *chudan*,

Illus. 203

Illus. 204

Illus. 205   Illus. 206

Illus. 207

jodan, or double punch *jodan-chudan (rentsuki)*—according to the opponent's guard. During the foot attack, the weightbearing leg must remain bent, the upper torso erect, and the kicking foot must immediately be brought back to the knee of the weightbearing leg.

Repeated Attack Technique

Another possible combination is to attack with the same technique immediately after the first attack. This can be with *tsuki* or *keri*. Your opponent must parry your first attack with a momentary tension. Immediately thereafter comes a phase in which his guard is weak. Turn this to your advantage by immediately springing the same attack towards the same target. A similar tactic is to attack once or twice not very quickly, then suddenly attack the same target with lightning speed. During the slow attacks, he is lulled into a false sense of security and is taken by surprise in the lightning-swift repeat that follows.

Throwing Opponent Off-Balance and Attacking

Ashi-barai (foot sweep) attack technique

Powerfully sweep aside *(barai)* the opponent's forward leg with your sole, preferably hitting him just above the ankle bone (Illus. 208). In doing this, be sure that the power for this sweeping movement of the leg comes from the hip and

Illus. 208

Illus. 209

Illus. 210

Illus. 211

that the upper part of your body is not too close to your opponent, who may then be able to reach you with *tsuki*. Sweep swiftly and powerfully with your leg! If this manoeuvre should cause him to fall, follow immediately with a technique (Illus. 209 shows a punch to the temple)—either *tsuki* or *keri* (stamping kick with the heel). Usually, however, this tactic only knocks the opponent off balance. This can be taken advantage of immediately with a *mawashi-geri* (Illus. 210 and 211). Note how Master Toyama protects himself with his left arm against possible counterattack (Illus. 211).

Ashi-barai/Tsuki (Illus. 212 and 213)

With the leg-sweep (Illus. 212), throw the body forward and, upon setting the forward leg down, *oi-tsuki* to the face (Illus. 213). You can also attack with *gyaku-tsuki* after *ashi-barai*.

Illus. 212   Illus. 213

Fumi-komi (stamping kick)

Instead of the leg-sweep, you can attack with the same foot with *fumi-komi* in order to throw the opponent off balance. (Illus. 214 shows a stamping kick with the outer edge of the foot; Illus. 215, with the sole of the foot.) *Fumi-komi* is advised against an opponent who stands somewhat sideways.

Illus. 214

Illus. 215

Knocking Aside Opponent's Guard and Attacking

The opponent's guarding arm is briskly knocked aside with the edge of the hand. This action must take place with lightning speed in the form of a direct thrust and

Illus. 216

Illus. 217

Illus. 218   **Illus. 219**

Illus. 220

not of a swing. This can be effectively executed especially when the opponent holds his guard somewhat away from his body. Knock his arm away inwards and downwards. This will tend to throw him off-balance (Illus. 216). Immediately attack with *tsuki* (Illus. 217) or *keri* (Illus. 218).

Instead of knocking the opponent's guarding arm aside, you can also seize it, thereby throwing him off-balance and then, immediately attack. One way of seizing the guarding arm is to execute *jodan-tsuki*. As the opponent blocks (Illus. 219), immediately open the attacking hand, let it drop and then yank the opponent off-balance, perpendicular to the line between his feet. Attack with *tsuki* (Illus. 220) or *keri*.

This is a combination from the examination program for the 2nd Kyu degree (blue belt). Try to carry through the entire combination smoothly, without stopping or interruption.

Illus. 221

Illus. 222

Illus. 223

Illus. 224

Illus. 225

Mawashi-geri/Uraken/Gyaku-tsuki (Illus. 226 to 230)

This combination is similar to the *Mawashi-geri/Ushiro-geri/Uraken/Gyaku-tsuki* series only without *ushiro-geri*. Upon setting down the kicking leg in *mawashi-geri*, execute *uraken* and then, without interruption, *gyaku-tsuki*.

Another situation leading to attack is when the distance between you and your opponent does not yield any more room for leg techniques and yet is not close

Illus. 226

Illus. 227

Illus. 228   **Illus. 229**   **Illus. 230**

enough for arm techniques. In this case, leave the upper part of your body in the same place but push your front foot slowly forward, your weight on your back leg. Now you can hurl your body forward with complete surprise by shifting your weight and attacking with *tsuki*.

V. Counter-Techniques

Up to now, we have been concerned with techniques for one's own attack. In fighting, however, you must also be in a position not only to ward off your opponent when he attacks but also to execute a counterattack immediately. For this reason, it is extremely important to engage in counter-techniques.

The most important movement in counter-technique, that is defence in connection with a counterattack, is the movement of the hips.

By means of a well-mastered hip movement you can let the attack take place without stopping its movement, therefore preventing the attacking energy from being consumed in your blocking members and causing injury. In this way, you are in a more advantageous position for the following counterattack, as you can make use of the opponent's own attack impetus for yourself. In defence, therefore, do not just retreat, but also move aside from the hips. In defence and moving aside, it is best to slip as far as possible to one side so that you are out of reach of your opponent's other hand. Moreover, in moving aside, you slip into the outer edge of his field of view.

Counter-Techniques Against Foot Attacks

To begin with, counter-techniques against foot attacks are of greater importance than those against arm techniques, as the fight must be opened from a greater distance with *keri*. The following techniques, therefore, are also recommended even when the actual attack is to be executed with *tsuki* but where the opponent makes use of a foot technique at the opening. In these techniques your movements are such that while unleashing a leg technique, your opponent cannot attack you with an arm technique at the same time.

Mae-geri, Kata-uke, Gyaku-tsuki (Illus. 231-233)

Move left to the side and somewhat forward, with a sharp hip movement upon setting down the left leg (Illus. 231). This way, the opponent's foot passes by and does not harm you even when it connects. Simultaneous with the turning of the hips, thrust the back of your forearm inwards to throw the opponent off-balance.

Illus. 231   **Illus. 232**

Illus. 233

You end up facing the opponent sideways (Illus. 232). With the return action of the hips, execute *gyaku-tsuki* (Illus. 233).

The following example shows how important the turning of the hips is in fighting. In Illus. 234, you see an attack with *mae-geri* which hits the target, but, at a right angle. In this way, the entire oncoming energy is absorbed by the target and the one struck is hurt. In Illus. 235, however, the target turns his hips sharply and displaces

Illus. 234   **Illus. 235**

his weight somewhat forward. As a result, the foot attack sweeps past him without doing any harm. Even when the target is struck in the course of this, nothing happens because the direction of the force is not pointed into his body.

Nagashi-tsuki

Master Toyama shows in *jiyu-kumite* this turning from the hips in very smart and lithe fashion. *Nagashi-tsuki* was developed from this hip turn which allows the attack to pass by. The turning away of the entire body from the hips becomes even more powerful with the back leg moving away at the same time. From this, still another principle evolves—at the moment the opponent's foot technique comes to rest, your body, the target, is no longer there.

When an opponent strikes at you with a stick, run in under it in order to relegate the danger (even at its greatest), to points way outside or beyond you. Similarly, in *nagashi-tsuki*, the forward leg glides towards the opponent, placing you out of the danger zone. By turning away the hips and setting back the rear leg, the attack passes harmlessly even while the rear leg is still in motion (see Illus. 236). At the same time, let go with *tsuki* as your counterattack. Illus. 237 and Illus. 238 show quite beautifully the entry into an attack. By this, the attacker is thrown over his weightbearing leg by the force of the entry. For safety, you can also make a left *gedan-barai* in countering *mae-geri* in conjunction with turning the hips away (Illus. 239-240).

Illus. 236

Illus. 237

Illus. 238

Motion picture studies of a big Japanese championship contest show that in attack techniques about 30 per cent of all attacks were carried out with *kizami-tsuki/gyaku-tsuki*. Another 30 per cent consisted of *kizami-tsuki/mae-geri* combinations. All other attacks were single cases, except for a direct attack with *mae-geri*. In counter-techniques, 55 per cent of all cases were merely retreats, without defence. In 15 per cent of the defence actions, defence was undertaken while retreating. Of the attacks, 30 per cent were blocked and at the same time the whole body was hurled forward in counterattack with *gyaku-tsuki*. This 30 per cent should interest us here.

Illus. 239   **Illus. 240**

Mae-geri/Gedan-barai/Gyaku-tsuki

The foot attack is warded off from the inside with *gedan-barai* (Illus. 241 and 242). The counterattack with *gyaku-tsuki* takes place immediately, while the attacking leg of the opponent is still in the air (Illus. 243). In such a position, he is still moving towards you, and both your speeds add together to make the counterattack highly effective. Moreover, so long as your opponent has his leg still in the air his balance is disturbed and he cannot ward off your counterattack. However, if he has already set his foot down again, he may be able to execute a strong immediate defence Therefore, against leg attacks, counterattack while the attacking leg is still in the air! In blocking the attack, keep a firm stance and as much as possible keep from giving ground. Most of all, do not shift the center of gravity, and in the *gyaku-tsuki* that follows, throw the entire body forward.

Illus. 241   **Illus. 242**   **Illus. 243**

Defence from the Outside

Here, sweep the foot attack from the outside towards the inside and enter into the attack somewhat left forward and thereby turn the hips away (Illus. 244; compare with page 86). Here, too, throw the bodyweight far forward against the counterattack and turn the hips all the way back into the *gyaku-tsuki*, before the opponent can set down his attacking leg (Illus. 245).

We conclude with yet another counter-technique against *mae-geri*. Here you stand in a right forward position and also defend from the outside. The back leg is pushed backwards and turned sideways (Illus. 246). At the same time, right *gedan-barai*, in connection with a powerful turning downwards of the hips and shifting of the weight to the left (Illus. 247). Immediately thereupon, turn the hips back inwards and bring through the left leg with *gyaku-tsuki*. Illus. 248 shows the preparation for the counterattack.

Illus. 244

Illus. 245

Illus. 246

Illus. 247

Counter–Techniques Against Fist Attacks

Here, too, the principle of defending as much as possible from the outside and coming sideways near or behind the opponent with the hip-turn and body-movement in order to execute the counterattack from that position is appropriate. It is especially important to execute the counterattack as simultaneously as possible. It is better to execute the counterattack at the same time as the defence, since the opponent offers an opening through his attack which must be taken advantage of immediately. For this reason, you must not retreat in the course of defence but stand fast or even enter into an attack.

An example of counter-techniques against fist attacks is *age-uke* and simultaneous *gyaku-tsuki* (Illus. 249). This simultaneous defence must be well-

Illus. 249

91

Illus. 250

Illus. 251

practiced, left and right. Defence and counterattack must be equally powerful. Enter into the opponent's attack with a parry from the inside and at the same time *gyaku-tsuki*. The opponent might, by way of example, attack with *kizami-tsuki/gyaku-tsuki* or *kizami-tsuki/mae-geri* (Illus. 250). As you block, enter into the attack and *gyaku-tsuki* (Illus. 251). Run both movements together. Practice a lot!

In another technique, *kake-uke*, the back of the fist of the blocking arm is brought to the left ear. The attacking arm is thereby shunted off as it hits the back of the forearm. Illus. 252 shows how to parry left with *kake-uke* and at the same time counter with *gyaku-tsuki*. This defence occurs in the *kata tekki* No. 1.

Illus. 252

Common to all these counter-techniques against fist attacks is the action of entering defensively into the opponent's attack and at the same time executing the counterattack. However, only by running both movements together will you be able to prevent the attacker from hindering your counterattack.

92

Counter-Techniques Against Ashi-Barai

The attack with a sweep of the foot is a very effective opener. The simplest defence against this is to shove the attacking leg aside (Illus. 253). Should the opponent be brought somewhat forward because of this, you can immediately counter with *yoko-geri*. If the opponent does not sweep powerfully enough and as a result stands with his upper body too near, you can counter immediately with *jodan-kizami-tsuki*.

However, if your weight is on the forward leg and the opponent manages to

Illus. 253

Illus. 254

Illus. 255

Illus. 256

Illus. 257

sweep it powerfully away, you cannot avoid falling down. To save the situation, immediately lift the attacked leg above his sweeping leg and "fall" down on him. With the momentum of your "falling" body, you are able to throw him off-balance (Illus. 254) and gain the possibility of following up immediately with *tsuki*.

Should your opponent succeed in sweeping your forward leg aside though not hard enough to make you fall, place it down immediately to the side towards which he swept (Illus. 255 and Illus. 256) and turn quickly on this leg with *ushiro-geri* (Illus. 257).

A Last Word on Free-Style Fighting Tactics

If a karateka lays more of an offensive fighting style on an opponent, the latter should employ a more waiting kind of fighting tactic. For this reason, some karatekas might be tempted to use attacking combinations while others, more counter-techniques. However, it is necessary for the karateka with the waiting style of fighting to concern himself also with attack combinations. He should keep in mind that only one contest is ever scheduled between two karateka who fight only in waiting style and who depend only on counter-techniques!

VI. The Kata

The so-called *kata* consists of a number of defence and counterattack techniques which are directed against four to eight imaginary attackers who "attack" from different directions and in numerous ways. They include the arm and leg techniques of defence, and attack from twisting, turning and leaping. In the 1930's, before the possibility of safe contests was recognized, the *kata* represented the highest form of karate. They were demonstrated extremely close to reality; the karateka actually "saw" his attacker whose attack he had to ward off and against whom he executed his tough, precisely-aimed counterattack.

Most *kata* had been practiced by old karate masters for a long time so that many of them are very old, though some date from more recent times. Out of them was developed modern karate and today are referred to as the "dictionary" of the art. There are about 50 *kata*, simple as well as very complicated ones. Some are plain and simple breathing exercises while others require cat-like adroitness.

A person can practice the *kata* alone, wherever there is sufficient room. By the multiplicity of techniques employed taken from every imaginable situation, they represent an extremely variable form of practice. They are not to be considered separate from modern karate, which is directed more towards competitive matches. In the *kata*, all the basic techniques are used in purer, more exact and more powerful form from within the movement, a practice which even from the viewpoint of free-style fighting, is very valuable. "*Kata* is the grammar, free-style fighting is the sentence."

Since the *kata* is usually organized in such a way that several opponents "attack" in different ways from different directions, they also represent a good practice for self defence.

Practice Tips

The *kata* is always an organic whole and must be learned and executed as such. The connection between defence and attack must be there. You must actually "see" your opponent and carry out your attack in order to show the near reality of *kata*. Many regard the *kata* only as a string of the most exact possible techniques and thus demonstrate them as such. Done this way, however, the *kata* does not "live." Such practitioners induce in the watcher none of the excitement that could lead to a better appreciation of the perfection of the techniques.

Every *kata* has a dynamic rhythm, with both rising and descending parts. The prerequisite for demonstrating the near reality of *kata* is naturally certainty in the round of movements. Not until you no longer have to think hard about the individual movements is your mind free to express the true spirit of the *kata*. For this reason, even while you are a beginner, practice *kata*. With the smoothening of your basic techniques, your *kata* becomes stronger and more exact and, at the same time, the round of movements becomes a part of your very flesh and blood. However, do not at that point remain complacent; rather, always try to bring life into *kata*. Always imagine an opponent and how swiftly and fiercely he attacks. In addition, always look at the imaginary attacker, keeping him within your glance. Also, you should know what every movement of the *kata* means in actual use. Make every movement clear to yourself as there are often several possibilities of meaning. Not until you know what you are doing can your *kata* have truth and hence come alive.

In all *kata*, the starting point and the ending point must coincide (see Illus. 258 and 281). The course of every *kata* is, as has already been noted above, precisely established. For every *kata*, a step-diagram can be laid out. Many *kata* are executed in a straight line, while other diagrams look like an H or a T, or they construct complicated figures.

Here, I shall describe the five so-called *heian-kata*. These *kata*, presented in *Shotokan* style, contain all the techniques of modern karate. Before Gichin Funakoshi changed them to today's form, they were distinguished by the Chinese name *ping an*, probably named after the master who created them. For this reason, they are required in the *karate-kyu* (student) examinations. Moreover, the *kata* *tekki* No. 1 *(nai hanchi)* is also represented, so that in this book we have the *kata* for everything—from the entire examination program up to and including the master black belt.

Heian Shodan (No. 1)

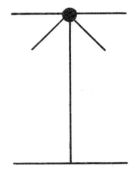

1. *Gedan-barai* to the left to ward off a foot attack (Illus. 259).
2. Advance with *oi-tsuki* (counterattack) (Illus. 260).

3. Execute a 180° turn by taking a step with *gedan-barai* using the left leg as the turning point (Illus. 261).

4. Pull the forward leg back to a natural right-forward position. At the same time, swing the right fist close to the left ear in an arc, then smash it downwards on the little-finger side. The opponent may have been able to grab your wrist after the left *gedan-barai*. By means of the back step, in conjunction with the arching movement, pull the opponent off-balance towards you thus freeing your hand, and smash him on the head with the fist in *tettsui-uchi*. Another interpretation of *tettsui-uchi* for blocking a following fist attack is seen in Illus. 262.

5. Now left forward with *oi-tsuki* (Illus. 263).

6. Turn 90° with *gedan-barai* (Illus. 264).

7. Advance in *zenkutsu-dachi* with *age-uke*. In doing this, raise the left hand high with open palm *(age-uke)* immediately at the beginning of the forward movement (Illus. 265). Now, advance with *age-uke*, bringing the left hand to the hip (Illus. 266). Another interpretation: Grab the attacker's arm with your left hand and pull him towards you. Lift your right forearm high to strike the opponent's arm at the elbow joint to break it.

8 and 9. Advance left and then right with *age-uke* (Illus. 267 and 268). In doing this, open the fist at the start of each new step. In number 9 (Illus. 268), shout *kiai* (the battle cry). Here is the strongest point in the defence because of the forcible exhalation in shouting *kiai*. Stop briefly.

10. Make a 90° turn on the right foot with *gedan-barai* defence (Illus. 269).

11. Immediately counterattack right forward with *oi-tsuki* (Illus. 270).

Illus. 258   **Illus. 259**   **Illus. 260**

12. Turn about 180° on the left foot, take a step and *gedan-barai* right (Illus. 271).
13. Immediately *oi-tsuki* in a leftward advance (Illus. 272).
14. Turn 90° on the left leg with *gedan-barai* (Illus. 273).
15 to 17. Advance three times with *oi-tsuki* (Illus. 274 to 276). On the third *oi-tsuki*, unleash your strongest attack with *kiai*. Hold briefly.
18. Turn 90° on the right leg into *kokutsu-dachi* with *shuto-uke* (Illus. 277). A tip for this turn: Leave the weightbearing leg sharply bent. Feel forward with the ball of the left foot and then turn the body as a unit into *kokutsu-dachi* with *shuto-uke*. This way, you can strike powerfully with *shuto-uke* out of the turn.

Illus. 261

Illus. 262

Illus. 263

Illus. 264   Illus. 265   Illus. 266   Illus. 267   Illus. 268

98

Moreover, you immediately stand without loss of balance in a low *kokutsu-dachi*. In all turns, hold yourself erect—power in the *hara*—otherwise you will lose your balance in the fast turns.

19. Advance with the right leg at a 45° angle (Illus. 278), *shuto-uke* in *kokutsu-dachi*. This can also be construed as a counterattack arising out of *shuto-uke*.

20. Now turn 135° to the right with *shuto-uke* (Illus. 279).

Illus. 269

Illus. 270

Illus. 271

Illus. 272

Illus. 273

Illus. 274

Illus. 275   **Illus. 276**   **Illus. 277**

21. Move left front at a 45° angle with *shuto-uke* (Illus. 280). Hold yourself briefly in the final position. Then, calm and relaxed, withdraw the left leg back to the starting position, inhaling while doing so (Illus. 281).

Illus. 278   **Illus. 279**   **Illus. 280**   **Illus. 281**

Heian Nidan (No. 2)

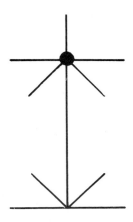

1. Shove the left leg leftward to *kokutsu-dachi* and, at the same time, ward off a fist attack from the left (Illus. 282 to 284).
2. For the next movement (Illus. 285), there are two possible interpretations. To start each one, the left fist is so sharply drawn back that its back is quite close to the right ear.
   First interpretation: Ward off a second fist attack, which the opponent now executes with his left fist. The movement of your left arm would thus be a kind of *soto-ude-uke* from the inside. At the same time, punch with the right fist in *ura-tsuki* towards the opponent.
   Second interpretation: Ward off the fist attack also with the left arm. However, strike with the right arm from outside against the opponent's elbow joint to break his arm.
3. Now, *tettsui-uke* to the solar plexus (Illus. 286).

4 to 6. Repeat the aforementioned movements using the other side of the body (Illus. 287 to 289).

7. Pull up the left leg a half-step at the same time, give a quick glance to the right, and in doing so, lay the right fist upon the left (Illus. 290).
8. Now the right, non-weightbearing leg is lifted (Illus. 291) and released into *yoko-geri-ke-age* with *uraken-uchi* at the same time. Another interpretation: Parry a fist attack to the side with *uraken*, at the same time counter with *yoko-geri* (Illus. 292).
9. Set the kicking leg down in *kokutsu-dachi* with *shuto-uke* and at the same time look around and turn the body about 180° (Illus. 293).
10. and 11. Advance right, then left in *kokutsu-dachi* with *shuto-uke* (Illus. 294 and 295).
12. Move right forward in *zenkutsu-dachi*, and *tate-nukite* to the solar plexus with *kiai*. In doing this, place the back of the left hand under the elbow of the thrusting arm (Illus. 296).

13 to 16. Execute the same steps as 18 to 21 in *Heian Shodan* (No. 1) (Illus. 297 to 300).

17. Place the left leg forward and to the left with only the ball of the foot touching the ground, thereby stretching both arms sideways (Illus. 301). Then swing the right arm through to a position under the left armpit (Illus. 302), so that the "stopping point" of the *uchi-ude-uke* right defence coincides with the completion

Illus. 282

Illus. 283

Illus. 284

Illus. 285

Illus. 286

of the leg movement and shifting of the bodyweight from *kokutsu* to *zenkutsu-dachi*. In doing this, swing the right hip forward (Illus. 303).

18. Advance with *mae-geri* right (Illus. 304).
19. Break off to *zenkutsu-dachi* with *gyaku-tsuki* (Illus. 305).
20. Thereupon, immediately heave the punching arm over the right shoulder into an *uchi-ude-uke* left, simultaneous with a powerful counter-turn of the hips (Illus. 306). In preparing for *uchi-ude-uke*, let the right fist remain either at the

Illus. 287   Illus. 288   Illus. 289
Illus. 290   Illus. 291   Illus. 292

hip and draw the left arm back over the right shoulder; or stretch the right arm out forward in a basic school manner and then swing the left fist over to a position under the right armpit.

21. Now, *mae-geri* left (Illus. 307).
22. and 23. Without a pause after the breaking off of *gyaku-tsuki* right (Illus. 308), *zenkutsu-dachi* right forward with *morote-uraken-uchi* attack or *morote-uke* defence (Illus. 309).

Illus. 293   Illus. 294   Illus. 295   Illus. 296   Illus. 297

Illus. 298   Illus. 299   Illus. 300   Illus. 301

24. Now turn 90° on the right leg with *gedan-barai* (Illus. 310), the left hand open and the left arm lifted high (Illus. 311).
25. Step 45° right forward in *zenkutsu-dachi* with *age-uke* (Illus. 312).
26. Turn 135° on the left leg with *gedan-barai* (Illus. 313).
27. Proceed 45° left ahead with *age-uke* and *kiai* (Illus. 314). Hold briefly, then draw the left leg back to *hachiji-dachi* (Illus. 315).

Illus. 302   **Illus. 303**   **Illus. 304**

Illus. 305   **Illus. 306**   **Illus. 307**

Illus. 308　　　　**Illus. 309**　　　　　　**Illus. 310**

In the *Heian Nidan* (No. 2), the difficult defence with the edge of the hand occurs no less than seven times. Also very difficult are steps 7 and 8, the *yoko-geri* with simultaneous *uraken-uchi*. In this, arm and leg must be as nearly parallel as possible while the other fist remains at the hip. The counter-turn of the hips in the defences of *uchi-ude-uke* in the *gyaku*-form (see Illus. 303 and 306) must be clearly visible.

Illus. 311　　　　**Illus. 312**　　　　**Illus. 313**

Illus. 314　　　　**Illus. 315**

Heian San dan (No. 3)

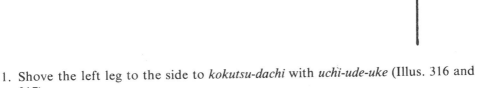

1. Shove the left leg to the side to *kokutsu-dachi* with *uchi-ude-uke* (Illus. 316 and 317).
2. Pull up the right leg to *heisoku-dachi* (feet together), at the same time, *uchi-ude-uke* and *gedan-barai*. In regard to this, a tip on method: When pulling up the right leg, stretch the right arm forward and bring both arms together so that the elbow of the left arm is laid on the elbow bend of the right arm (Illus. 318). Immediately, without interruption and with this resting place as a turning point, *uchi-ude-uke* with your right arm and *gedan-barai* left (Illus. 319).
3. Now do the same in reverse (Illus. 320).

4. Turn about 180°. Shove the right leg forward to *kokutsu-dachi* and *uchi-ude-uke* (Illus. 321).

5 and 6. Correspond to steps 2 and 3 (Illus. 322 and 323).

7. Turn 90° to the left. Shove the left leg forward to *kokutsu-dachi* with *morote-uke* (Illus. 324).

8. Step right forward in *zenkutsu-dachi* with *nukite*, as in *Heian Nidan* (No. 2) (Illus. 325).

9. (Illus. 326 to 328). Interpretation of this movement: the opponent has gripped your punching arm by the wrist and pulls backwards on it. Bend forward in a yielding way, and in doing so turn your hand with the palm upwards (Illus. 326). As you now pull in the left leg past, and close to, the weightbearing leg, turn your gripped hand on its back and twist it from the opponent's grip (Illus. 327). Now, move the left leg towards the opponent in *kiba-dachi* and smash him at the same time with *tettsui-uchi* in the solar plexus as you come out of the turn (Illus. 328).

10. Conclude with *oi-tsuki* in a right forward move with *kiai* (Illus. 329).

11. Shove the left leg ahead to *heisoku-dachi* and, in doing so, turn your body about 180°. Plant your fists firmly to your sides (Illus. 330). Glance back to the starting point, then following the direction of the glance, go back to that point.

12. Ward off a right fist attack with *mikatsuki-geri-uke* from the inside (Illus. 331).

13. Set the leg down with *fumi-komi* (stamping kick) in the opponent's knee-bend, at the same time warding off another fist attack with *kata-uke*—the attacking arm is fended off towards the inside with the upper arm (Illus. 332).

14. *Uraken-uchi* right to the opponent's head with an immediate snapping back of the fist to the hip (Illus. 333).

15 to 17. Repeat movements 12, 13 and 14 using the left side of the body (Illus. 334 to 336).

18 to 20. Do the same movements using the right side of the body once more (Illus. 337 to 339).

21. Poise the left fist in the starting position for a fist punch. At the same time, stretch the right palm forward with a relaxed arm (Illus. 340) and shoot an *oi-tsuki* left forward (Illus. 341).

22. In a circular movement, align the right leg with the forward leg (Illus. 342). With the right leg as a turning point, make a 90° turn to *kiba-dachi* and out of the turn, whip a left elbow punch to the rear at the opponent who has been standing behind you with the intention of grabbing you into a stranglehold. Follow up with *tate-tsuki* to his face (Illus. 343).

23. Concluding immediately in *kiba-dachi*, slide to the left, unleash an elbow punch and a fist punch to the side with *kiai* (Illus. 344). After a brief hold in the relaxed final position, assume a loose starting stance, shoving the right leg forward. In doing this, inhale again to relax.

Illus. 316   **Illus. 317**   **Illus. 318**

Illus. 319   **Illus. 320**   **Illus. 321**   **Illus. 322**

Illus. 323   Illus. 324   Illus. 325   Illus. 326   Illus. 327

Illus. 328   Illus. 329   Illus. 330   Illus. 331

Illus. 332

Illus. 333

Illus. 334

Illus. 335

111

Illus. 336

Illus. 337

Illus. 338

Illus. 339

Illus. 340

Illus. 341

Illus. 342

Illus. 343

Illus. 344

Heian Yo dan (No. 4)

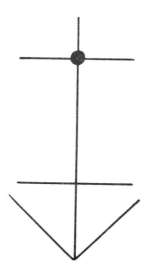

1. This defence is similar to the first moves in *Heian Nidan* (No. 2), only here the hands are held open (Illus. 345 to 347). Also, in *Heian* No. 2, this defence is quickly snapped upwards. Here, however, the hands are brought upwards slowly, taking about 5 seconds. Tension is thus increased so that in the final position of this first movement (Illus. 347), you are in a state of higher tension.
2. Turn on the spot and assume the same stance (Illus. 348).
3. Bring the left leg forward (Illus. 349), turn 90° with a long step forward in *zenkutsu-dachi*. In doing this, bring the hands back from the right to the rear in preparation for *gedan-juji-uke* or defence against the initial stage of a foot attack. Cross the right fist over the left and hold both fists vertically (Illus. 350).
4. Step right forward in *kokutsu-dachi* with *morote-uke* (Illus. 351).
5. Glance to the left and pull the left leg forward (Illus. 352). *Yoko-geri* and *uraken* as in *Heian Nidan* (No. 2) step 8 (Illus. 353).
6. Snap the kicking foot back to the knee of the weightbearing leg, then set it down in *zenkutsu-dachi* with *gyaku-empi-uchi*, jabbing the right elbow forward from the hip. In the *kata*, this is indicated by striking the entire back of the right forearm, fist held erect, against the inner side of the left forearm and the left palm (Illus. 354).
7 and 8. Repeat movements 5 and 6, using the other side of the body. Start by glancing to the right (Illus. 355 to 357).
9. Glance 90° to the left, at the same time *gedan-barai* with the edge of the left hand and *age-uke* with the edge of the right hand (imagine the opponent attacking right with a leg and left with a fist to the face) (Illus. 358). Effect a

swift and powerful shift in the body's center of gravity, from the right to the left leg, by means of the forceful passing through of the right leg. While doing this, give blows with the edge of the hand from the hip-turn to the right, along with *age-uke* to the left (Illus. 359). All these mean that the opponent, who has attacked right with the leg and left with the fist, continues to attack, even after your defence, by placing a kick to your face along with a fist punch to the right. Deflect this movement to the left with *age-uke* and execute the *shuto-uchi* counterattack to the right against his temple. The whole manoeuvre must be carried out in one continuous movement.

10. In precisely the same direction (against the same opponent), *mae-geri* right (Illus. 360).
11. Upon setting down the kicking leg which has been shoved far forward by the bent, weightbearing leg, grip the opponent's arm with the left hand and yank him towards you. Strike out with the right fist over the left shoulder or the head (Illus. 361) to *uraken-uchi* to the chin or solar plexus (Illus. 362). Another way of using the left hand in this situation is to press down a fist attack with it *(osae-uke)*. In doing so, hook the ball of the left foot behind the right upon setting down the right leg *(kake-dachi)*, and *kiai* at the same time. Hold briefly.
12. Set the left leg at a 45° angle to its previous position and wedgeblock *(kakiwake-uke)* against an opponent who tries to grip your clothing with both hands or attacks with *morote-tsuki*. Thereby, the arm crossed over the wrist is held at the level of the chin (palm towards the face, the right fist open). Then, strike both arms downwards, and away from each other to produce the wedge effect, to the position shown in Illus. 363 and Illus. 367—arms bent, the elbows not projecting sideways from the body.
13. Advance with *mae-geri* right (Illus. 364).
14. When setting the foot down in the same direction, *oi-tsuki* (Illus. 365).
15. Immediately *gyaku-tsuki* (Illus. 366). In doing this, don't bring the punching hand to the hip during the previous *oi-tsuki*.
16. Turn on the left leg about 90° and thereupon, 45° to the original direction (Illus. 367).
17 to 19. Repeat positions 13 to 15 (Illus. 368 and 369).
20. Set the forward (left) leg back again at a 45° angle to the line of the original attack, to *kokutsu-dachi* with *morote-uke* (Illus. 370).
21 and 22. Advance right, then left with *morote-uke* (Illus. 371 and 372).
23. Throw the bodyweight forward to *zenkutsu-dachi* in order to set the forward leg sideways at shoulderbreadth. Thereby, you can grab the opponent's head with both hands, fingertips at the back of the skull (Illus. 373).
24. Yank his head down against your swiftly rising knee and *kiai* (Illus. 374).
25. Immediately set the kicking leg down, at the same time, turn 180° with *shuto-uke* (Illus. 375).
26. Finally, go right forward with *shuto-uke* (Illus. 376). Hold this position briefly,

then quietly bring the forward leg back to *hachiji-dachi*. The direction of the glance remains the same (Illus. 377).

Illus. 345   **Illus. 346**   **Illus. 347**

Illus. 348   **Illus. 349**   **Illus. 350**   **Illus. 351**

Illus. 352

Illus. 353

Illus. 354

Illus. 355

Illus. 356

Illus. 357

Illus. 358

Illus. 359

Illus. 360

Illus. 361

Illus. 362

Illus. 363

Illus. 364

Illus. 365

Illus. 366

Illus. 367

Illus. 368

Illus. 369

Illus. 370

Illus. 371

Illus. 372

The *Heian-kata* No. 4 consists of all the most important attack punches, blows and steps and also the most important defences, turns, weightshifts from the hips, and so on. For this reason, it is the most universal among the five *Heian-kata*. Also in positions 14 and 15 as well as in 18 and 19, the double-punch *(rentsuki)* is used for the first time. It is required in karate-*kyu* examinations for the 3rd *kyu* degree (green belt).

Illus. 373

Illus. 374

Illus. 375

Illus. 376　　　　　　**Illus. 377**

Heian Godan (No. 5)

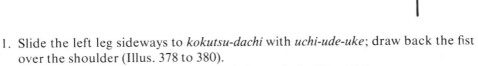

1. Slide the left leg sideways to *kokutsu-dachi* with *uchi-ude-uke*; draw back the fist over the shoulder (Illus. 378 to 380).
2. Counterattack with *gyaku-tsuki* from *kokutsu-dachi* (Illus. 381).
3. Draw the back leg forward to *heisoku-dachi*. Simultaneously, put your right fist near your hip and describe the movement of a *kagi-tsuki* with the open left hand which, in the final position, is closed into a fist. Turn your glance to the right. This movement is executed in a very relaxed manner (Illus. 382).

4 to 6. Repeat positions 1 to 3 using the right side of the body and directing the final glance straight forward (Illus. 383 to 385).

7. Advance right in *kokutsu-dachi* with *morote-uke* (Illus. 386).
8. Advance left in *zenkutsu-dachi* with *juji-uke (gedan)* (Illus. 387).
9. Immediately thrust your open hands high to *juji-uke (jodan)* (Illus. 388).
10. Turn the crossed hands around each other at the wrists (Illus. 389), then draw the right hand back to the right hip and close it tightly. Hold the left hand open out front (Illus. 390).
11. Advance with *oi-tsuki* (Illus. 391).
12. Turn on the left leg about 180° with *mikatsu-geri-uke* right (Illus. 392), striking off the fist attack to the right with the sole of the foot. Simultaneously, strike out with the right fist into *gedan-barai* and, upon landing, block a subsequent foot attack (Illus. 393).
13. Turn a glance and slowly execute *haishi-uchi* which is a blow with the back of the hand thought to be a defence against a fist attack (Illus. 394 and 395).
14. Now counterattack with *mikatsuki-geri*. In doing this in the *kata*, strike the sole of the foot against the palm of your outstretched hand (Illus. 396). Thereupon, immediately set the foot down to *kiba-dachi* and attack several times with elbow punches right forward. As in *Heian Yo dan* (No. 4) steps 6 and 8, the back of the punching right forearm must strike against the inner side of the left forearm and palm (Illus. 397).
15. Glance to the right, cross the left leg behind and *morote-uke* (Illus. 398). Most karateka prefer to execute this as *chudan-morote-uke*. The picture shows its execution as *jodan*-defence.
16. Place the left leg to the left, glancing in that direction and energetically thrusting both hands high (break away). In doing this, the left foot should point to the left and should be set down only on the ball of the foot (Illus. 399).
17. Leap in the direction of the glance (Illus. 400) as the opponent attempts to strike your leg with a long stick. Upon landing with the left leg crossed behind the right, block a subsequent foot attack with *juji-uke*. Your stance need not be as low as shown in Illus. 401. It is also important to keep your back straight.
18. Glance to the right, advance towards that direction in *zenkutsu-dachi* with *morote-uke* (Illus. 402).
19. Turn 180° on the spot into *zenkutsu-dachi*. Set the rear leg about two shoulderbreadths to the right, then turn the body and shift the weight to the ball of the foot. Another interpretation: An opponent attacks in position 18 with a fist punch (*oi-tsuki* right) from behind. By turning and then warding off the punch with the palm of the left hand *(nagashi-uke)*, you enter into the attack and can then deliver a right *nukite* (fingertips) or *shotei* (heel of the hand) to his abdomen (Illus. 403).
20. Place the forward leg a shoulderbreadth towards the middle and return the bodyweight to *kokutsu-dachi*. Simultaneously, left *gedan-barai* against a foot attack and right *uchi-ude-uke (jodan)* against a fist attack from behind (Illus. 404). Another interpretation: After having punched the opponent in the

abdomen with the right hand (position 19), grab hold of him with the same hand and by a combination of pulling, dragging down with your bodyweight, and side pressure with your left arm, make him fall. Sweep his forward leg aside by setting your forward leg towards the inside.

Illus. 378

Illus. 379

Illus. 380

Illus. 381

Illus. 382

Illus. 383

21. Slowly pull up the forward leg to *heisoku-dachi* (Illus. 405).
22. Take a right step forward in *zenkutsu* and deliver a left *nukite* or *shotei* to your opponent's abdomen (Illus. 406). Then, immediately set this forward leg towards the middle, bringing the bodyweight back to *kokutsu-dachi* with *gedan-barai* and *uchi-ude-uke* (Illus. 407). Hold briefly, then bring the forward leg back to the starting position.

Illus. 384

Illus. 385

Illus. 386

Illus. 387

Illus. 388

Illus. 389

Illus. 390

Illus. 391

Illus. 392

Illus. 393

Illus. 394

Illus. 395

Illus. 396

Illus. 397

Illus. 398

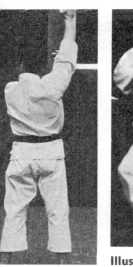

Illus. 400

Illus. 401

Illus. 402

Illus. 399

Illus. 403

Illus. 404

Illus. 405

Illus. 406

Illus. 407

Tekki No. 1 (Nai hanchi)

In the three *tekki kata* you move only in a straight line and always in *kiba-dachi*. For this reason, a diagram is not needed here. *Tekki 1* is required in the examination for the first *kyu*-degree.

1. Starting position: *Heisoku-dachi*. Lay the fingertips of the left hand over those of the right, thumb folded in (Illus. 408).
2. Glance to the right, simultaneously crossing the left leg over the right (Illus. 409).
3. Raise the right leg in a high arc (Illus. 410) while warding off a back-of-the-hand blow at the same time (Illus. 411).
4. *Empi-uchi* left as in *Heian Yo dan* (No. 4) and *Heian Godan* (No. 5)—counterattack (Illus. 412).
5. Glance to the left, simultaneously placing the left fist over the right fist and lodging both of them on the right hip (Illus. 413).
6. *Gedan-barai* left (Illus. 414).
7. Follow up with *kagi-tsuki* (Illus. 415).
8. Again, cross the legs (Illus. 416) with a swift, upwards movement of the left leg. At the same time, turn the glance forward and heave your right arm over your left shoulder.
9. *Uchi-ude-uke* immediately upon landing (Illus. 417).
10. Now, in one unchanging pace, *gedan-barai* right, *kake-uke* left (Illus. 418), then

Illus. 408   **Illus. 409**   **Illus. 410**

immediately counterattack with *uraken-uchi* (or *ura-tsuki*) to the opponent's chin. In doing this, hold the back of the right fist under the elbow joint of the attacking arm (Illus. 419).

11. Glance to the left towards where the opponent might sneak in a foot attack. Strike off the attacking leg towards the inside with the sole of the foot *(nami-ashi)* (Illus. 420), and ward off the subsequent fist attack with the left forearm (Illus. 421).

12. Repeat number 11 using the right side of the body (Illus. 422 and 423).

Illus. 411

Illus. 412

Illus. 413

Illus. 414

13. Look to the left, fists one atop the other and both poised from the right hip (Illus. 424).

Illus. 415

Illus. 416

Illus. 417

Illus. 418

Illus. 419

Illus. 420   Illus. 421   Illus. 422

Illus. 423   Illus. 424

Illus. 425   **Illus. 426**

14. Thrust both fists to the left. The left fist defends while the right shoots a *kagi-tsuki* which the opponent runs right into (Illus. 425).
15. Give a slow blow with the back of the hand *(haishi-uchi)* (Illus. 426 and 427).

Illus. 427   **Illus. 428**

Illus. 429   **Illus. 430**

16. From here on, execute the exact reverse (Illus. 428 to 438) of the first part of *Tekki* No. 1 (Illus. 412 to 425). Following each cross-over step, whip the leg upwards in a wide arc and set it down forcefully in a swift movement. Following the reverse application of Illus. 425 (Illus. 437), slowly draw up the right leg towards the left, into the starting position (Illus. 438).

Illus. 431   **Illus. 432**   **Illus. 433**

Illus. 434

Illus. 435

Illus. 436

Illus. 437

Illus. 438

VII. Karate As Self Defence

Karate has, of course, been known longest as a means of self defence. A big advantage of karate as a sport, as it is practiced today, is that it does not lose sight of this serious aspect, even in harmless contests. In a real fighting situation, sport karate can be turned into an effective self defence without adding anything further which, for example, is only relatively true for *judo* as a sport. The same karate techniques learned in karate as a sport, can be used against an armed or unarmed opponent.

In real situations of distress, karate can be a very rough and dangerous kind of defence. For this reason, not every attack warrants a defence with karate attack techniques. Usually, it is sufficient to carry out a strongly executed karate defence,

Illus. 439

e.g., a block against an attacker. Owing to the severe pain which the attacker then experiences, he will probably desist at once from further attack. Thus, in a relatively harmless attack such as an attacker's simple attempt to grab a hold on a victim, one need not and should not reply with a karate counterattack. Naturally, in attacks involving a brutal fighter or dangerous weapons, one need not hesitate to unleash the power of karate as self defence. In such serious circumstances, foot techniques, the use of which provides a very great degree of surprise, are strongly recommended.

Well-practiced karate techniques, especially when one has already had experience in sport contests, make it possible for one to meet any attack with self-confidence, or to run away. It does not, however, make one invincible! Hence, do not be too sure of yourself! Always recognize the fact that your antagonist is dangerous!

In Illus. 439, Master Toyama demonstrates a simultaneous defence against two attackers. The fist punch of the attacker on the left is warded off to the left with *kake-uke* at the same time that a fist punch is delivered to the chin. Simultaneously, a *yoko-geri-kekomi* is slammed to the breast of the other antagonist.

VIII. Kuatsu—The Art of Resuscitation

Kuatsu, already several hundred years old, rests on the stimulation of the nervous system by means of special massage applied on certain nerve centers.

Sensitive Body Spots

Karate techniques are always directed against sensitive body spots. This is an important principle to pay attention to if one's defence against a dangerous attacker is to be effective. Moreover, knowledge of sensitive body spots is also an important principle in karate sport contests, which is this book's main concern. In fact, in karate sport contests, only such techniques are subject to evaluation as would, in a real case, put the antagonist immediately out of the fight—the so-called *chi mei*. As target points in a match, the following areas are specified:

(a) the head, except for the eyes

(b) the neck, except for the larynx

(c) the trunk: in front, from the nipples down to the genitalia; behind, from the spinal column to the loins and the side areas above the loins.

It sometimes happens in sport contests that a karateka comes up against an opponent who has an uncontrolled technique. It is important that every practice instructor be informed of this and of where the nearest physician is to be found. Also, the instructor should have available the phone number of the Fire Department Emergency Squad or an ambulance service. It is noteworthy, however, that serious accidents seldom occur in karate. Nevertheless, it would be useful to describe effective measures for the most frequent kinds of karate accidents.

1. A Blow or Kick in the Groin (Illus. 440)

In minor cases, it is enough for the injured contestant to repeatedly massage the middle of the flexure of the groin with his fingertips. If the pain is more severe, one should strike the rumpbone or sacrum (the spot indicated in Illus. 441) with the heel of the hand or, if the man is sitting, with the ball of the foot.

If because of a blow, the testicles are pressed upwards into the abdominal cavity,

Illus. 440

Illus. 441

Illus. 442

grasp the sitting man under the shoulders first, then lift him up a little bit and ease him down on the floor again. Do this repeatedly until the testicles have returned to their natural position. Following this, strike the rumpbone as described above. A second person may also massage the groin region (Illus. 442), using the sides of his hands to knead the flexure of the groin.

The best prevention against groin injury is to wear a cup (groin protector).

2. A Kick in the Stomach, Liver, Solar Plexus or Lower Abdomen (Illus. 443)

The characteristics of this type of injury are pain and cramping in the farthest possible bent position of the spinal column (Illus. 444). Plant the knee firmly against the spine, grasp the shoulders (Illus. 445) and stretch the spine forcibly (Illus. 446). The cramp is thereby released. Bring the muscles back to normal tension by massaging the stomach with the sides of the hands (Illus. 447).

3. Loss of Consciousness

In cases of groin and stomach injuries, the pain can be so severe as to cause the loss of consciousness. For this, artificial respiration in accordance with various methods is the best immediate treatment. In doing this, be sure that the tongue does not fall back into and block the air passages. If it does, it must be pulled back out at once.

Another treatment, especially for cases involving heart-stoppage and interruption of breathing, is the stimulation of the vegetative nervous system—here

Illus. 443

Illus. 444

Illus. 445

Illus. 446

Illus. 447

the solar plexus—in order to revive heart action and breathing. Lay the unconscious victim on his back, bare his breast and abdomen and spread his arms out at right angles to his body, his palms facing up. Kneeling at his right side, place the right palm on his breastbone, the forearm slanting outwards at about a 45° angle. Now slide this hand downwards until the palm lies in the hollow of the stomach. At this point, push with the hand's heel against his body in the direction of the forearm. Push in the rhythm of the heartbeat, about 60 times a minute.

Consciousness can also be restored by forcefully striking the unconscious victim's bare sole, particularly the arch, with your balled fists. This is for the stimulation of the peripheral nervous system. When consciousness has returned, help the patient to a sitting position and have him make a large circle over his breast with his arms. Finally, with you supporting, he should stand up and walk around to normalize his blood circulation.

4. Nosebleed

A wild blow against the nose can cause it to bleed. In such a case, let the patient sit down, lay your left hand lightly on his head and with the edge of the right hand strike lightly three or four times against the nape just above the hairline. Finally, lay his head slightly backwards, then grasp his neck with the right hand just above the shoulder. With the flat of the left hand, strike a few oblique blows lightly to the forehead. This should be so executed that the hand slides off the forehead at each blow. Strike three or four times, then let him sit for a minute.

Appendix

Suggested Regimen for Karate Training

		Minutes
I.	Gymnastics	
	Warming-Up and Stretching Exercises	5
II.	Basic School *(Kihon)*	
	1. *Tsuki:* Proceed with *oi-tsuki, gyaku-tsuki*	10
	2. *Keri:* Proceed with *mae-geri, yoko-geri, mawashi-geri*	10
	3. Combinations	10
III.	Practice with Partner *(Kumite)*	
	1. In accordance with stage of proficiency, practice *ippon-kumite*, fighting combinations, or counter-techniques in freer form	10
	2. *Jiyu-kumite* (free style fighting)	20
IV.	*Kata*	20
V.	Loosening-Up Exercises, Massage	5
		90

Plan your training in such a way that arduous exercises are alternated with those that require more thinking or with those that do not take so much strength as is called for in many stretching exercises. The introduction of new techniques can also serve this purpose.

Here is another suggestion for a plan for a beginner's course. Train in two-hour periods twice a week for three months.

1st WEEK

Monday: Fist-punch from *hachiji-dachi*
 Mae-geri from *hachiji-dachi*
 Zenkutsu-dachi and movements in this stance
Friday: Repeat Monday's exercises
 Oi-tsuki
 Mae-geri combined with *zenkutsu-dachi*

2nd WEEK

Monday: Repeat Friday's exercises
 Gyaku-tsuki (interpretation of the hip-turn)
 Yoko-geri from *hachiji-dachi* (foot action)
 Kiba-dachi and movements in this stance
Friday: Repeat Monday's exercises
 Proceed with *oi-tsuki* and *gyaku-tsuki* and with *mae-geri*
 Proceed with *yoko-geri* in *kiba-dachi* from the crossing of the legs and the turn
 Proceed with *yoko-geri* in *zenkutsu-dachi*

144

3RD WEEK

Monday: Repeat Friday's exercises
Mawashi-geri from *zenkutsu-dachi* with a partner standing in a fixed position
Gedan-barai from *zenkutsu-dachi*

Friday: Repeat Monday's exercises
Mawashi-geri proceeding with *zenkutsu-dachi*
Gedan-barai proceeding with *zenkutsu-dachi*
Proceeding with *gedan-barai* and concluding with *gyaku-tsuki*
Kokutsu-dachi

4TH WEEK

Monday: Repeat Friday's exercises
Proceed with *oi-tsuki, gyaku-tsuki* (double punch)
Proceed with *mae-geri . . . gyaku-tsuki*
Soto-ude-uke
Shuto-uchi (blow with the edge of the hand)

Friday: Repeat Monday's exercises
Proceed in *zenkutsu-dachi* with *soto-ude-uke . . . gyaku-tsuki*
Shuto-uke in *kokutsu-dachi*

5TH WEEK

Monday: Repeat Friday's exercises
Age-uke, the basic form from *hachiji-dachi*
Ushiro-geri, the basic form

Friday: Repeat Monday's exercises
Proceed with *age-uke . . . gyaku-tsuki*
Ushiro-geri

6TH WEEK

Monday: Repeat Friday's exercises
Combination of defence and attack in partner-practice (see Illus. 135-140). *From now on, carry out this exercise on every training night!*
Ippon-kumite
Attack *chudan-tsuki . . . soto-ude-uke . . . gyaku-tsuki*

Friday: Repeat Monday's exercises
Attack *mae-geri . . . gedan-barai . . . gyaku-tsuki*
Empi-uchi (upwards)

7TH WEEK

Monday: *Ippon-kumite:* attack *chudan-tsuki . . . soto-ude-uke* from inside . . . *shuto-uchi*

145

Attack *jodan-tsuki . . . age-uke . . . gyaku-tsuki* and *empi-uchi*
Empi-uchi to the side

Friday: Repeat Monday's exercises
Ippon-kumite: attack *chudan-tsuki . . . soto-ude-uke* from inside . . . *shuto-uchi*
Attack *jodan-tsuki . . . age-uke . . . shuto-uchi*
Attack *mae-geri . . . gedan-barai* from outside . . . *jodan gyaku-tsuki*

8TH WEEK

Monday: Repeat Friday's exercises
Uchi-ude-uke
Proceed with *shuto-uke* in *kokutsu-dachi*
Sanbon-kumite, three successive attacks or defences
Chudan-tsuki . . . soto-ude-uke . . . gyaku-tsuki
Jodan-tsuki . . . age-uke . . . gyaku-tsuki
Mae-geri . . . gedan-barai . . . gyaku-tsuki

Friday: Repeat Monday's exercises
Proceed with *uchi-ude-uke . . . gyaku-tsuki*
Ippon-kumite: attack *chudan tsuki . . . uchi-ude-uke* from *kokutsu-dachi*
Counterattack with *gyaku-tsuki* from *zenkutsu-dachi*
Sanbon-kumite

9TH WEEK

Monday: Repeat Friday's exercises
Proceed with *shuto-uke* in *kokutsu-dachi . . .* change over to *zenkutsu-dachi* with *gyaku-tsuki*
Sanbon-kumite

Friday: Repeat Monday's exercises
Proceed with mae-geri . . . gyaku-tsuki
Ippon-kumite: attack *jodan-tsuki . . . juji-uke . . . mae-geri*
Empi-uchi forward

10TH WEEK

Monday: Repeat Friday's exercises
Proceed with *mae-geri . . . mawashi-geri*
Ippon-kumite: attack *jodan-tsuki . . . age-uke . . . empi-uchi* forward
Sanbon-kumite

Friday: Repeat Monday's exercises
Jiyu-ippon-kumite
Sanbon-kumite
Uraken-uchi

11TH WEEK

Monday: Repeat Friday's exercises
              Proceed with *uraken-uchi . . . gyaku-tsuki*
              Sanbon-kumite
              Jiyu-ippon-kumite
              Hittsui-geri (knee kick)

Friday: Repeat Monday's exercises
              Jiyu-kumite (cover, distance apart)

12TH WEEK

Monday: Repeat Friday's exercises
              Only *tsuki, keri* and *uke*
              Kata Taikyoku 1 (see "Karate: Basic Principles")

Friday: Repeat Monday's exercises
              Examination of individuals with discussions
              Jiyu-kumite

Examination Rules for Karate-Kyu and Dan Degrees

Note: F = Forward
     B = Backwards
     S = Sideways

yoi = attention
kamaete = command to assume starting position
hajime = fight, begin
mawatte = turn
naotte = relaxed basic stance
yame = stop, end

6th Karate-Kyu Degree (White Belt)

1. *Dojo*-etiquette (ceremonial)
2. Commands (see Note)
3. Attack stages *(jodan/chudan/gedan)*
4. *Kihon* (basic techniques)
   (a) F: *Zenkutsu-dachi* with *gedan-barai*
   (b) F: *Kokutsu-dachi* with *age-(jodan)-uke*
   (c) S: *Kiba-dachi* with *gedan-uke* (sideways)

The starting position *for all techniques* in *zenkutsu-dachi* is *zenkutsu-dachi* left forward with *gedan-gamae*.

5th Karate-Kyu Degree (Yellow Belt)

In *kihon*, techniques executed together are basically to be executed fluidly, one after the other. The arm techniques must be stopped. All defence techniques end in *"Hanmi."* At the final technique in a series, carry this out with *Kiai*.

1. *Kihon*
   Tsuki and *uke*
   (a) F: *Zenkutsu-dachi/oi-tsuki*—turn with *gedan-barai*
   (b) F: *Zenkutsu-dachi/gyaku-tsuki*—turn with *age-(jodan)-uke*
   (c) F: *Zenkutsu-dachi/age-(jodan)-uke*—turn with *uchi-uke*
   (d) F: *Zenkutsu-dachi/uchi-uke, gyaku-tsuki*—turn with *uchi-uke*
   Keri
   (a) F: *Zenkutsu-dachi/mae-geri*—turn in *kiba-dachi*
   (b) F: *Kiba-dachi/*cross-over step *yoko-geri-keage*
   (c) F: *Kiba-dachi/*cross-over step *yoko-geri-kekomi*
2. Combinations
   (a) *Mae-geri/gyaku-tsuki*
   (b) *Mae-geri/jodan-chudan-rentsuki*

Entire combinations are to be brought out from a free-style attack position. In *tsuki*, the punching fist starts out from the position of readiness and immediately springs back.

3. *Kumite*
   (a) *Sanbon-kumite (jodan* and *chudan)*
   (b) *Kihon-ippon-kumite (jodan* and *chudan* alternating)
   Every *kumite* form is evaluated separately.
4. *Kata*
   Heian (Pinan) Shodan (No. 1)
End of 5th Karate-Kyu Degree (Yellow Belt)

4th Karate-Kyu Degree (Orange Belt)

1. *Kihon*
   Tsuki and *Uke*
   (a) F: *Zenkutsu-dachi/oi-tsuki*—turn with *gedan-barai*
   (b) F: *Zenkutsu-dachi/sanbon-rentsuki*—turn in *kokutsu-dachi* with *shuto-uke*
   (c) F: *Kokutsu-dachi/shuto-uke, gyaku-tsuki* in *zenkutsu-dachi*
   (d) B: *Zenkutsu-dachi/soto-uke, gyaku-tsuki*
   Keri
   (a) F: *Zenkutsu-dachi/mae-geri*—turn in *zenkutsu-dachi*
   (b) F: *Zenkutsu-dachi/mawashi-geri*—turn in *kiba-dachi*
   (c) S: *Kiba-dachi*/turn, with back leg *yoko-geri-keage*
   (d) S: *Kiba-dachi*/turn, with back leg *yoko-geri-kekomi*
2. Combinations
   (a) *Yoko-geri/gyaku-tsuki*
   (b) *Yoko-geri/uraken/gyaku-tsuki*
3. *Kumite*
   (a) *Kihon-ippon-kumite (jodan* and *chudan* alternating)
   (b) *Jiyu-ippon-kumite (jodan-* and *chudan-tsuki)*
4. *Kata*
   Heian (Pinan) Nidan (No. 2)
End of 4th Karate-Kyu Degree (Orange Belt)

3rd Karate-Kyu Degree (Green Belt)

1. *Kihon*
   Tsuki and *Uke*
   (a) F: *Zenkutsu-dachi/sanbon-rentsuki*
   (b) B: *Zenkutsu-dachi/uchi-uke, gyaku-tsuki*
   (c) F: *Zenkutsu-dachi/soto-uke*, change over to *kiba-dachi/yoko-empi/uraken*
   (d) B: *Kokutsu-dachi/shuto-uke, gyaku-tsuki* in *zenkutsu-dachi*
   Keri
   (a) F: *Zenkutsu-dachi/mae-geri-rengeri* (same leg *chudan, jodan)*—turn in *kiba-dachi*
   (b) S: *Kiba-dachi*/cross-over step, *yoko-geri-age*, turn, with back leg *yoko-geri-kekomi*—turn in *zenkutsu-dachi*

(c) F: *Zenkutsu-dachi/mawashi-geri*
2. Combinations
   (a) *Mae-geri (jodan)/mawashi-geri (chudan)/yoko-geri-keage*
   (b) *Mawashi-geri/ushiro-geri/uraken (jodan)/gyaku-tsuki (chudan)*
3. Kumite
   (a) *Kihon-ippon-kumite (jodan-, chudan-tsuki* and *keri* every second time)
   (b) *Jiyu-ippon-kumite (tsuki* and *keri)*
4. *Kata*
   Heian (Pinan) San dan (No. 3)
End of 3rd Karate-Kyu Degree (Green Belt)

2nd Karate-Kyu Degree (Blue Belt)

1. *Kihon*
   Tsuki and *Uke*
   (a) F: *Zenkutsu-dachi/Sanbon-rentsuki*
   (b) B: *Zenkutsu-dachi/uchi-uke, kizami-tsuki, gyaku-tsuki*
   (c) F: *Zenkutsu-dachi/soto-uke*, change over in *kiba-dachi/yoko-empi, uraken*
   Keri and *Tsuki*
   (a) F: *Zenkutsu-dachi/mae-geri-rengeri*—turn in *kiba-dachi*
   (b) S: *Kiba-dachi*/cross-over step, *yoko-geri-keage*, turn, with back leg *yoko-geri-kekomi*—turn in *zenkutsu-dachi*
   (c) F: *Zenkutsu-dachi/mawashi-geri, gyaku-tsuki*
2. Combinations
   (a) *Kizami-tsuki/mae-geri (chudan)/jodan-chudan-rentsuki*
   (b) *Mawashi-geri/uraken, gyaku-tsuki/mae-geri/jodan-chudan-rentsuki*
3. *Kumite*
   (a) *Kihon-ippon-kumite*
   (b) *Jiyu-kumite*
4. *Kata*
   Heian (Pinan) Yo dan (No. 4)
End of 2nd Karate-Kyu Degree (Blue Belt)

1st Karate-Kyu Degree (Brown Belt)

1. *Kihon*
   Tsuki and *Uke*
   (a) F: *Zenkutsu-dachi/sanbon-rentsuki*
   (b) B: *Zenkutsu-dachi/uchi-uke, kizami-tsuki, gyaku-tsuki*
   (c) F: *Zenkutsu-dachi/soto-uke*, change over in *kiba-dachi/shuto-uchi, gyaku-tsuki* in *zenkutsu-dachi*
   (d) B: *Kokutsu-dachi/shuto-uke, mae-geri* with forward leg/*gyaku-tsuki* in *zenkutsu-dachi*

(e) *Zenkutsu-dachi/gyaku-tsuki* against given target

Keri and *Tsuki*

(a) F: *Zenkutsu-dachi/mae-geri-rengeri*—turn . . .

(b) F: *Zenkutsu-dachi/mae-geri* and *yoko-geri-kekomi* (same leg), *gyaku-tsuki*—turn . . .

(c) F: *Zenkutsu-dachi/mae geri* and *mawashi-geri* (same leg), *gyaku-tsuki*

2. Combinations

(a) *Mawashi-geri/yoko-geri-kekomi/ushiro-geri/uraken (jodan)/gyaku-tsuki (chudan)*

(b) *Mae-geri* and *yoko-geri* (same leg), *gyaku-tsuki/mae-geri* and *mawashi-geri* (same leg), *gyaku-tsuki*

3. *Kumite*

(a) *Jiyu-ippon-kumite*

(b) *Jiyu-kumite*

4. *Kata*

(a) *Heian (Pinan) Godan* (No. 5)

(b) *Tekki (Nai hanchi)* No. 1

5. Knowledge of contest rules

6. Knowledge of first aid

End of 1st Karate-Kyu Degree (Brown Belt)

1st Karate-Dan Degree (Black Belt)

1. Knowledge of the entire examination program for *Karate-kyu* degrees.

2. *Kihon*

(a) F: *Zenkutsu-dachi/sanbon-rentsuki*

(b) B: *Zenkutsu-dachi/age-(jodan)-uke-gyaku-tsuki*

(c) F: *Zenkutsu-dachi/uchi-uke, kizami-tsuki, gyaku-tsuki*

(d) B: *Kokutsu-dachi/shuto-uke, mae-geri, gyaku-tsuki* in *zenkutsu-dachi*

(e) F: *Zenkutsu-dachi/mae-geri-rengeri*

(f) F: *Zenkutsu-dachi/mawashi-geri*

(g) S: *Kiba-dachi/yoko-geri-keage*

(h) S: *Kiba-dachi/yoko-geri-kekomi*

(i) F: *Zenkutsu-dachi/mawashi-geri, yoko-geri-kekomi*

(k) F: *Zenkutsu-dachi/mawashi-geri* and *yoko-geri-kekomi* with the same leg

3. Combinations

(a) F: *Mae-geri* and *yoko-geri-kekomi* (same leg), *uraken, gyaku-tsuki, mawashi-geri, gyaku-tsuki* (left and right)

(b) Standing in place: *Kizami-tsuki/F: oi-tsuki/B: gedan-barai, mae-geri* (with forward leg), F: *Mawashi-geri, uraken, gyaku-tsuki*

4. *Kumite*

(a) *Jiyu-ippon-kumite*

(b) *Jiyu-kumite*

5. Karate defence against attacks with weapons
6. *Kata*
   Free (not from the *kyu* degree examination program)
7. Mastery of contest rules, in theory and practice
8. Knowledge of first aid
End of 1st Karate-Dan Degree (Black Belt)

2nd Karate-Dan Degree (Black Belt)

1. Knowledge of the entire examination program through 1st *Karate-dan.*
2. *Kihon*
   Insofar as no starting position is prescribed, it can be freely chosen.
   (a) F: *Kizami-tsuki, sanbon-rentsuki*
   (b) F: *Kizami-tsuki*, slide forward leg to the front and *mae-geri, oi-tsuki* with back leg
   (c) S: *Kiba-dachi/yoko-geri-keage*, turn, *yoko-geri-kekomi* with back leg
   (d) B: *Age-(jodan-)uke, mawashi-geri* with back leg, *uraken* in *kiba-dachi,* one step forward with *oi-tsuki* in *zenkutsu-dachi*
   (e)   *Mae-geri, yoko-geri-kekomi* with back leg
3. Combinations
   (a) Remaining in place with one leg (left and right). *Mae-geri* forward, *yoko-geri-kekomi* sideways, *ushiro-geri* backwards, *mawashi-geri* forward
   (b) B: *Age-(jodan-)uke* and *soto-uke* (same arm), F: *mae-geri-sanbon-rentsuki,* B: *uchi-uke, gyaku-tsuki*
4. *Kumite*
   (a) *Jiyu-kumite*
5. Karate defence against attacks with weapons
6. *Kata*
   Free (not from the *kyu* degree examination program)
7. Mastery of contest rules in theory and practice
8. Knowledge of first aid
End of 2nd Karate-Dan Degree (Black Belt)

Glossary of Japanese Karate Terms

Age or *Ago*—rising
Age-tsuki—rising blow or uppercut
Age-uke (Jodan-uke)—upwards block (rising blow with fist or hand)
Ashi—leg
Ashikubi—ankle
Ashi-no-ko—instep
Ashiura—sole of the foot
Ashiwaza—leg and foot techniques
Ashizoko—bottom of the foot
Atemiwaza—methods of attacking vital spots in the body

Chokusen-kata—straight line *kata*
Choku-tsuki—direct thrust
Chudan—defence of the middle level of the body
Chudan-soto-uke—middle outside block with forearm
Chudan-tsuki—middle thrust or punch
Chudan-uchi-uke—middle inside block with forearm

Empi—elbow punch
Engisen—demonstration line

Fudodachi—immobile posture
Fukushiki kumite—double contest *kata*
Fumikiri—step out
Fumi-komi—foot stamping technique
Fumi-tsuki—stamping on opponent's instep
Fumi-uchi—step blow
Furi-tsuki—swinging thrust or blow

Gedan—defence of the lower level of the body
Gedan-barai—downwards parry
Gedangamae—attack position (as in *gedan-barai*)
Gedan-tsuki—lower step or body blow
Gedan-uke—lower step or body block
Gohon-kumite—partner practice with five consecutive attacks (see *sanbon-kumite*)
Gorei—word of command
Gyaku—reverse
Gyaku-tsuki—reverse punch

Hachiji-dachi—basic stance
Haishi-uchi—blow with the back of the hand
Hajime—begin, fight
Hara—lower abdomen
Haraite—sweeping hand
Hasen-kata—wave-line *kata*
Heiko-dachi—parallel stance
Heisoku—instep
Heisoku-dachi—stance with feet together
Hiho—secret formula, method, etc.
Hiji—elbow
Hijiate—elbow attacks
Hiza—knee
Hizagashira—knee-cap
Hiza-geri—knee kick
Hizatsui—knee hammer

Jiyu-ippon-kumite—semi-free sparring form (only one attack)
Jiyu-kumite—free-style contest
Jodan—defence of the upper level of the body
Jodan-tsuki—upper body blow
Jodan-uke—upper body block
Juji-uke—crossblock
Jun-tsuki—side thrust or punch

Kagi-tsuki—hook punch
Kakato—heel
Kakato-geri—heel kick
Kakewake—thrust aside
Kamaete—command to take attack position
Kanzetsu-geri—kick to the knee
Karateka—practitioner of karate
Kata—prescribed karate demonstration form
Kata-shiai—demonstration tournaments
Keage—high forward kick
Kentui-uchi—striking techniques
Keri—kick
Kerigaeshi—return kick
Kerihanashi—kick release
Kerikomi—kick in
Keri-waza—kicking techniques
Kiai—battle cry

Kiba-dachi—straddle-leg stance
Kihon—basic school
Kihon-ippon-kumite—basic school partner contest (only one attack)
Kime—focal point
Kizami-tsuki—punch without a focal point or *kime* used in preparation for an attack
Kobushi—fist
Ko-empi—rear elbow blow
Kokutsu-dachi—back stance
Ko-te—forearm
Kuatsu—ancient art of resuscitation
Kumite—practice with a partner (contest exercises)
Kyusho—vital spots in the body

Mae-geri—frontal kick
Mae-geri-keage—frontal kick using snapping motion of the knee
Mae-geri-kekomi—frontal kick with noticeable use of the hip
Mae-tobi-geri—foot attack from the air
Mawashi-geri—roundhouse kick
Mawashi-tsuki—roundhouse punch
Mawatte—turn
Morote-tsuki—punch with both fists
Morote-uke—block using one arm to support the other
Musubi-dachi—linked-feet stance

Nagashi-uke—sweeping parry
Nageashi—leg throw
Naotte—relaxed basic stance
Nekoashi-dachi—shortened back stance
Ni-dan-geri—foot attack from the air
Nukite—finger thrust

Oi-tsuki—lunge punch

Rengeri—double kick
Rentsuki—double punch
Renzokutsuki—continuous blows

Sanbon-kumite—partner practice with triple attack (contest exercises)
Sanbon-rentsuki—triple punch, once *jodan* and twice *chudan*
Seiken—normal fist
Seiken-choku-tsuki—straight punch with front of fist
Semete—assailant in *kata*

Shihan—master or teacher
Shotei—heel of the hand
Shuto-uchi—blow with edge of the hand
Shuto-uke—defence with edge of the hand
Soto-ude-uke—use of the outer edge of the forearm, fist down
Soto-uke—outside block
Sukuite—scooping hand

Tate-empi—vertical elbow thrust
Tate-tsuki—vertical punch
Tate-zaiki—straight punch with quarter turn of the fist
Te—hand
Tekubi—wrist
Tettsui-uchi—striking techniques
Tewaza—hand techniques
Tobi-geri—jumping kick
Tobi-goshi—jumping over
Tsuki—punch, thrust
Tsukite—punching hand

Uchi-uke—inside block
Ude—arm
Uke—block
Ukete—receiver in *kata*
Ukewaza—defence techniques
Uraken or *Riken*—back of the fist
Ura-tsuki—back of the fist striking techniques
Ushiro-geri—kick to the rear

Watsuki—circling blow

Yoko-empi—side elbow thrust
Yoko-geri—side kick
Yoko-geri-keage—side kick from the knee-joint that instantly snaps back
Yoko-geri-kekomi—side kick with powerful hip action
Yoko-tobi-geri—kick attack from a jump

Zen-empi—frontal elbow thrust
Zengo-empi—front and rear elbow thrust
Zenkutsu-dachi—forward stance

INDEX